WHAT THE FACT?!

365 STRANGE DAYS IN HISTORY

By GABE HENRY

Illustrations by DAVE HOPKINS

CHRONICLE BOOKS

SAN FRANCISCO

For Danny, Nora, and Celina

Several of the entries in this book originally appeared in
a different form on Mediander.com and have been revised
and republished here with permission from Michael J. Fine.

Library of Congress Cataloging-in-Publication Data
Names: Henry, Gabe, author.
Title: What the fact?! : 365 strange days in history / Gabe
Henry.
Description: San Francisco : Chronicle Books, 2018.
Identifiers: LCCN 2018014919 | ISBN 9781452168531
(hardcover : alk. paper)
Subjects: LCSH: History–Miscellanea–Calendars
Classification: LCC D11.5 .H46 2018 | DDC 904–dc23 LC
record available at https://lccn.loc.gov/2018014919

ISBN 978-1-4521-6853-1

Manufactured in China

Illustrations by Dave Hopkins
Design by Michael Morris

10 9 8 7 6 5 4

Chronicle Books LLC
680 Second Street
San Francisco, California 94107
www.chroniclebooks.com

THIS BOOK BEGAN WITH A SIMPLE FACT.

Years ago, while wandering the halls of the New-York Historical Society, I peered into a display case and beheld a page of notes from the journal of Pierce Butler, one of America's Founding Fathers. The date on the notes was May 1787—the first meeting of the Constitutional Convention—and the page was full of doodles.

As far as attention span goes, this South Carolina delegate seemed no less distractible than a bored high school student sitting through math class. Here he was, one of only a few men on hand to witness the birth of America, and he'd spent the hours doodling little squiggles, shapes, and portraits of men in powdered wigs. (Not very good portraits, either, I might add.) I felt my mouth forming the words then and there—*What the f . . .*

And so the seed was planted.

From then on, I was obsessed with finding strange archival

facts—quirky tidbits from the fringes of history that bring some humanity or humor to our picture of the past. I've since uncovered the police arrest records of Pablo Picasso, the window decorating habits of L. Frank Baum, and the X-rated letters of Mozart. I unearthed Lincoln's stellar amateur wrestling record (he lost only once) and Alexandre Dumas's pitiful dueling stats (he *won* only once). I even found a photo of Franklin Roosevelt in a dress.

I groped for years in libraries, hoping for a serendipitous discovery. I plundered the archives of the New-York Historical Society and the U.S. Patent Office. I tracked down dates in old ship ledgers. My collection of curiosities started to grow.

To give this random assortment some structure, I began ordering it by calendar date—one weird and wonderful factual delicacy per day of the year. The process turned from hoarding to purging, as I now had to exclude dozens, if not hundreds, of amusing stories from my collection that either I couldn't find a date for or that shared a date with an already existing entry. (Sadly, Pierce Butler never made it to the final draft.) My fellow hoarders out there know the pain. It was paralyzing.

Though I've done my best to check each story and date, a handful of the dates are inherently unverifiable, and for these I've had to rely on some academic guesswork. Regarding the story of John Howland and the *Mayflower* (October 1), for example, a museum librarian helped me to triangulate the date of the Atlantic storm by cross-referencing several documents, including the birth records of Oceanus Hopkins, the only child born on the *Mayflower* during its voyage to America. Using the scant evidence available, we narrowed our estimate for that fateful 400-year-old event down to October 1. But the truth is, only the *Mayflower* passengers would be able to confirm that for us. (For a list of sources used in this book, please visit GabeHenry.com.)

The book has plenty of strange material of more recent vintage as well. Here, too, is Tupac Shakur's high school ballet recital, Ozzy Osbourne's voracious appetite for live animals, the Swedish footballer who was ejected for breaking wind on the pitch, the 2017 film that made just £7 on its UK opening weekend, the Colombian actress who was sued by her own embryos, and other weird and entertaining stories from the modern era. What is history, after all, if not well-aged pop culture?

My greatest joy in writing this book has been watching it take on a life of its own. I found while arranging these oddities that many began to align according to theme, quite on their own, forming unexpected fellowships with surrounding entries. On May 23, 1618, an assembly of Protestants threw three noblemen out of a third-story window; on the next calendar date, May 24, 1920, the president of France fell out of a window on a moving train dressed only in his pajamas. Surely, some cosmic force decreed long ago that these two stories should one day line up back-to-back in a book of calendric miscellany.

I hope the cosmic force that brought these stories together has also brought you to this book. I'm sure you will find no less magic in the union.

THE BIG STINK
January 1, 1836

On New Year's Day 1836, a New York dairy farmer named Thomas Standish Meacham presented the President of the United States with an unusual gift: a 1,400-pound wheel of sharp, stinky cheddar.

Not quite sure what to do with it, President Andrew Jackson spent the next few months distributing the cheese in generous chunkfuls to his friends and fellow statesmen. When he wasn't serving it up at dinner parties, he kept it stored in a back vestibule in the executive mansion, where it built up its aroma for over a year.

Finally, in early 1837, as the overripe stench began to permeate into the furniture and fixtures, Jackson announced a public reception. He hauled the remaining cheddar into the main foyer of the White House, opened his doors, and invited everyone in the nation to come have a bite.

Ravenous visitors poured in by the thousands. "All you heard was cheese, all you saw was cheese, all you smelt was cheese," recalled one witness. "The whole atmosphere for half a mile around was infected with cheese."

By the end of the feast, there was cheese everywhere—coating the doorknobs, stamped into the carpets, wedged into the furniture cushions—and the smell lingered long after the last diner left. With only two weeks remaining in his presidency, Jackson didn't bother deodorizing. He let his successor worry about that: "[Martin Van Buren] had a hard task to get rid of the smell of cheese," wrote the wife of a Massachusetts senator, "and in the room where it was cut, he had to air the carpet for many days."

After battling the odor for weeks, Van Buren banned food from all future White House receptions.

THE HOLE TRUTH
January 2, 1953

If the nineteenth century was free and loose with its cheese, the twentieth century was anything but. Beginning in the 1920s, the United States Department of Agriculture began regulating everything from the percentage of pepper allowed in Monterey Jack to the proper placement of the word "smoked"—whether before or after the product name—on the packaging of smoked Gouda. On January 2, 1953, the government introduced yet another sweeping regulation—to the size of holes allowed in Swiss cheese. Henceforth, the "eyes" in a wheel of Grade A could each measure no more than half an inch wide, with similar reductions made to the other grades down to D. The new law also limited the number of holes in a given sample to eight.

THE CUTEST DIMPLES
January 3, 1996

One of the stranger accolades bestowed upon world leadership has to be *Cosmopolitan*'s honor to Nelson Mandela. On January 3, 1996, the glamor mag honored the 77-year-old anti-apartheid leader with its highest distinction—South Africa's sexiest and most eligible bachelor.

"He's everything a woman could ever want in a man," gushed the magazine, "mega-powerful, kind, modest, considerate and with a great sense of humor. Not to mention the cutest dimples."

The appreciation, it turns out, was mutual. During Mandela's political imprisonment on Robben Island, *Cosmo* was one of the few magazines allowed past prison censors. Inmates discovered they could send coded messages to the outside world via postcards indicating page numbers and word positions found inside the magazine. An abettor on the outside had only to scan the latest *Cosmo* to receive Mandela's message.

ELECTROCUTING AN ELEPHANT
January 4, 1903

As part of a smear campaign to discredit his rival, Nikola Tesla, Thomas Edison held a series of disturbing public animal electrocutions—a few stray dogs and cats, some cattle and horses, one orangutan—using Tesla's alternating current (AC), to demonstrate that it was more hazardous than Edison's direct current (DC). His biggest stunt occurred on January 4, 1903, when he zapped a Coney Island circus elephant named Topsy before a crowd of 1,500 spectators at Luna Park Zoo in New York. The 6,600-volt AC charge killed Topsy in seconds—and Tesla's public credibility along with it.

The stunt also served the Edison brand in another way: It helped promote his kinetoscope, an early motion picture device on which viewers could watch the brutal execution over and over again in the Edison-produced short *Electrocuting an Elephant.*

TOUCHÉ
January 5, 1825

Alexandre Dumas, the French author known for his sword-dueling epics *The Man in the Iron Mask* and *The Three Musketeers,* was no great duelist himself. On this day, the 22-year-old won his first and only sword duel when his opponent tripped over a tree root, fell backward into the snow, and surrendered.

Dumas emerged unhurt, though not without a deep psychological scar: During the fight his belt buckle broke and his pants fell down.

THE QUARREL IN 'MARLE
January 6, 1681

Boxing was a popular entertainment in Ancient Rome, but the sport died out about the time the empire did. It would be centuries before slugfests returned to European society as a spectator sport. The first recorded boxing match of the modern era took place on January 6, 1681, when Christopher Monck, the second Duke of Albemarle, orchestrated a bout between his butcher and his butler. The butcher came out on top, and so did his legacy: Since then, at least a dozen professional prizefighters have taken the mighty moniker "The Butcher" for a nickname, but no man dubbed "The Butler" has ever dared show his mug in the ring.

BUNNY MOTHER
January 7, 1964

On this day, the first service uniform was trademarked with the U.S. Patent Office: the Playboy bunny costume.

The formfitting satin corset with the fluffy cottontail, white collar, black bow tie, and rabbit ears was the official work uniform of servers at the Playboy Clubs from 1960 to 1988. Credit for the outfit goes to B-list TV actress Ilse Taurins, who in 1959 pitched her boyfriend, Playboy executive Victor Lownes, the idea of dressing the club's hostesses to match the rabbit logo of *Playboy* magazine. Ilse had her mother stitch the prototype.

CAMPAIGN PROMISE
January 8, 1835

At a lavish banquet in Washington, D.C., a Missouri senator stood up, clinked his glass, and proclaimed: "This month of January 1835, in the fifty-eighth year of the Republic, Andrew Jackson being president, the national debt is PAID!" Earlier that day, with a final installment of $33,733, the U.S. had wiped its national debt to zero. It was the only time that the country was debt-free.

By the following New Year's Day, the debt had already climbed back up to $37,000, and by January 1837 it was $337,000. Eager to keep his campaign promise of a debt-free America, President Jackson sold off western lands to speculators, but his impatience created a land bubble that eventually burst and led to one of the longest economic depressions in American history.

HONEST MISTAKE
January 9, 1493

On this day, Christopher Columbus spotted three aquatic creatures off the Dominican coast and mistook them for mermaids. He described them in his journal as "not half as beautiful as they are painted."

Scientists believe that most of history's mermaid sightings have actually been encounters with manatees, slow-moving mammals of the deep with bulbous bodies and humanlike eyes. In the right light and the wrong mind, the manatee's shape can be mistaken for the familiar female hourglass—especially to sailors who have gone months without seeing a woman.

WHERE'S THE BEEF?
January 10, 1984

Clara Peller, an 81-year-old manicurist from Chicago, Illinois, became an overnight sensation on January 10, 1984, when she appeared in a TV ad for the fast food chain Wendy's to deliver her now-classic catchphrase: "Where's the beef?"

She would find the beef months later in a jar of spaghetti sauce—and with Wendy's' lawyers—when the sprightly spokeswoman appeared in a TV spot for Prego proclaiming, "I found it! I really found it!" Wendy's abruptly terminated her contract, stating, "Clara can find the beef only in one place, and that is Wendy's."

MR. VERSATILITY
January 11, 1987

On this date, Ashrita Furman of Queens, New York, jumped underwater on a pogo stick in the Amazon River for three hours and forty minutes to become the Guinness World Record–holder for most Guinness World Records, with 119. (He has since upped the mark to around 200.) Furman's other records include slicing apples with a Samurai sword, catching ping-pong balls with chopsticks, and cutting potatoes while hopping on a shovel.

WHAT'S THAT SMELL?
January 12, 1960

In the 1950s, as movie theaters began losing customers to their home television sets, theater-owners came up with various gimmicks to put people in seats. This was the beginning of 3-D technology, as well as "Cinerama," a forerunner of IMAX in which three 35 mm projectors were pointed at one large, deeply curved screen. Some theaters even installed electric buzzers to shock audience members during moments of heightened action on-screen.

The most desperate—and disastrous—attempt to hype up movie-going was Smell-O-Vision, the life's work of Hans Laube, an expert in osmology from Zurich, Switzerland, who was driven into poverty by his failed invention. Smell-O-Vision pumped aromas, such as tobacco and fresh bread, into theater seats at precise moments during a film to accentuate plot points or build up suspense. (You could smell a villain coming around the corner.) The first and only SOV flick ever made, *Scent of Mystery,* premiered in Chicago on January 12, 1960, to a poor reception. Audience members complained that the odors were too faint, didn't coincide properly with the action on-screen, and that the loud sniffing of their neighbors made for a particularly unpleasant experience. Comedian Henny Youngman later quipped, "I didn't understand the picture. I had a cold."

GOVERNMENT SPY
January 13, 1999

Furby, the stuffed animatronic "it" toy of 1998, was the first plaything that actually became smarter as you played with it. Furby came out of its box speaking "Furbish," a goo goo gaga baby talk, but over time would "learn" human language (in this case English)—a process resembling language development in humans.

This development was simulated, of course: Furby came preprogrammed with all the words and phrases it was ever going to know. Nevertheless, a rumor spread that Furby's language-learning mechanism relied on hearing and imitating its owner—a fact that, if true, meant the must-have cyberpet of the late-nineties was actually a recording device. With Soviet espionage fears still lingering and the President of the United States currently undergoing impeachment due to a wiretap, the U.S. government naturally grew paranoid. On January 13, 1999, the National Security Agency announced a ban on all Furbies inside its headquarters for fear the furry little gremlins—whomever they were working for—might go blabbing national security secrets to the whole world.

SUE & DESTROY
January 14, 1999

On this date, Metallica filed a lawsuit against Victoria's Secret for trademark infringement, alleging that the women's lingerie company branded a line of lipstick "Metallica" without the band's authorization.

Metallica's hardcore image took another hit the following year when the French perfume maker Guerlain issued a special edition vanilla-based "Metallica" fragrance. The band slapped Guerlain with an infringement suit in December of 2000.

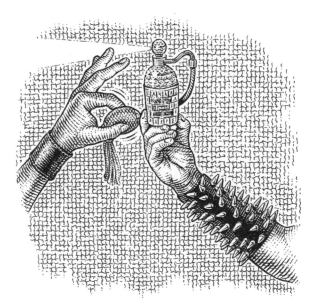

THE BOSTON MOLASSES DISASTER
January 15, 1919

On an unseasonably warm winter day in 1919, a molasses tank in Boston's North End exploded, sending a wave of thick black syrup tearing through the streets at 35 mph. It toppled buildings, crumpled railroad girders, and leveled a good part of the Boston waterfront. By close of day, the Boston Molasses Disaster had killed 21 people and injured 150 more.

The flood began at the Purity Distilling Company, a chemical firm specializing in the production of ethanol from molasses. The temperature in Boston had risen overnight from 2 to 40°F, which triggered fermentation inside one of the molasses tanks. As the goop bubbled, carbon dioxide pushed out against the walls. At around 12:30 p.m., witnesses in Keany Square heard a sound like rapid gunfire. The tank was shooting out rivets.

The 50-foot-tall, 90-foot-wide structure gave way at a weak spot near its base, and 2.3 million gallons of Puerto Rican molasses cascaded onto Commercial Street. It swallowed up people and horses like quicksand, hardening as it did. When rescue workers eventually cracked into the crystallized muck, they found victims frozen as in the ashes of Pompeii.

Cleanup crews took months to wash out all the molasses, and for years afterward streetcars, public telephones, and fire hydrants were still sticky to the touch. Even as late as the 1940s, locals claimed they could smell molasses on warm days.

JAMAICA MISTAICA
January 16, 1996

Jimmy Buffett isn't strictly a tequila man. Between margaritas on his porch swing in Key West, the laidback musician indulges in another island vice—marijuana. Buffett is keen on green, and for a short time in his early twenties he even made a living ferrying it from the Caribbean to Florida. He was a good smuggler—in the sense that he never got caught—but karma caught up to him twenty years later in an incident that has since become legendary in Buffett lore.

Buffett was taxiing his Grumman HU-16 airplane in the waters near Negril, Jamaica, on January 16, 1996, when the air cracked with gunfire. He and his guests (U2's Bono among them) dove for cover as the plane took hit after hit. The Grumman lost a windshield and a few bullet-sized patches of aluminum siding but, miraculously, its passengers emerged unscathed.

Narcotics agents on the Caribbean island had mistaken Buffett's craft for a drug-runner's plane. The Jamaican government publicly apologized, for fear Buffett—the unofficial spokesman for chill island living—would bring bad press to Jamaican tourism. Buffett ended up turning the story into a modest hit, "Jamaica Mistaica" (1996), without much damage to Jamaica's reputation.

JUST DO IT
January 17, 1977

When convicted killer Gary Gilmore faced the firing squad on January 17, 1977, he stood up tall and confident. "Let's do it," he said. Years later, a young Portland ad-man named Dan Wieden was struggling to write a motivational slogan for a fledgling athletic-wear company when Gilmore's words came to mind. He recalled:

> *"The night before the presentation I got worried the stuff didn't hang together enough. . . . So I sat down, I think it took me about 20 minutes, and I wrote four or five lines. . . . And for some damn reason I thought of Gary Gilmore."*

The next morning he delivered his proposal: Just Do It. Nike's slogan is based on the last words of a murderer.

BREAD BREAK
January 18, 1943

In the interest of wartime rationing, the U.S. banned all sliced bread effective January 18, 1943.

The War Department considered sliced bread a luxury, and preferred its steel resources be used for the barrels of guns rather than bread-slicing machines. A sliced loaf also required more wax paper than a non-sliced loaf, since bread goes stale quicker once it's carved up—and theoretically required more wheat as well, since stale loaves get thrown out sooner. Wheat, steel, and wax paper were all critical wartime resources.

The backlash was fierce and immediate. On January 26, *The New York Times* printed a letter from one agitated housewife:

> *I should like to let you know how important sliced bread is to the morale and saneness of a household. My husband and four children are all in a rush during and after breakfast. Without ready-sliced bread I must do the slicing for toast—two pieces for each one—that's ten. For their lunches I must cut by hand at least twenty slices, for two sandwiches apiece. Afterward I make my own toast. Twenty-two slices of bread to be cut in a hurry!*

Bakers and homemakers didn't have to stomach the ban for long. After two months of criticism, the U.S. government withdrew the order, admitting that the savings hadn't been as much as anticipated.

LUCY STICKS TO SCRIPT
January 19, 1953

In a strange intersection of real-life and fiction, Lucille Ball and Lucy Ricardo gave birth on the same day: Lucille first, at a Los Angeles hospital, followed hours later by her TV character, when the *I Love Lucy* episode "Lucy Goes to the Hospital" broadcast in homes across America. (Seventy-two percent of all American homes with televisions tuned in.) The next morning, the *New York Daily Mirror* ran the headline, "Lucy sticks to script: a boy it is!"

CBS had danced around Ball's pregnancy for months. The network had a rule that pregnant women could not be shown on-air; even the implication that television couples had sex was forbidden. (Lucy and husband Ricky had separate beds.) For their biggest star, however, they made an exception and agreed to write the pregnancy into the show, on one condition: Lucy would not be referred to as "pregnant" but rather "expecting." Or, in Ricky's English: "'spectin'."

REVENGE OF THE BATS
January 20, 1982

At a concert in Des Moines, Iowa, Black Sabbath front man Ozzy Osbourne bit the head off a live bat tossed onstage by a fan. (Ozzy claimed that he thought the bat was rubber, but he had also bitten the head off a live dove in the offices of his record company some months earlier.) The bat would have its revenge: The singer was later subjected to painful treatment for rabies at a local hospital.

Things weren't over yet between the Prince of Darkness and his nocturnal foe. In 2004, a family of long-eared bats took up roost in an old barn on Ozzy's Buckinghamshire estate. Thanks to the Wildlife and Countryside Act of 1981—an act established to protect wildlife from, among other things, predatory heavy metal singers—Ozzy had to pay more than $27,000 to have them removed before continuing with a planned renovation.

BEER AND BOILED APPLES
January 21, 1667

On this day, the first medical publication appeared in America—a one-page pamphlet on how to treat smallpox. The 12 x 17-inch broadside described the primitive treatment for this disease:

> *Let [the patient] drink small Beer only warm'd with a Tost, let him sup up thin water-gruel, or water pottage made only of Indian Flour and water, instead of Oat-meal: Let him eat boild Apples: But I would not advise at this time any medicine besides. . . .*

Smallpox treatment was due for a scientific breakthrough, to say the least. That breakthrough came exactly 122 years later, on January 21, 1799, when Dr. William Woodville of the St. Pancras Smallpox Hospital in London injected the first patient with a smallpox vaccination.

THE 334 CLUB
January 22, 1987

The New Jersey Devils expected some 12,000 fans at Meadowlands Arena for a regular-season hockey game against the Calgary Flames on January 22, 1987. A crippling blizzard prevented all but 334 from reaching the stadium.

Two weeks later, these 334 diehards received a letter in the mail: "You are hereby inducted and given lifetime membership to a club that cannot grow—the 334 Club." The letter was signed by Larry Brooks, the Devils' Vice President of Communications, and included a "334 Club" T-shirt, complimentary tickets, and a special VIP badge. "The Devils organization thanks you for your loyal support, which on the night of January 22, was certainly above and beyond the call of duty."

Membership in the 334 Club has since become a badge of honor among hockey fanatics—so much so, in fact, that the number of people who claim to have braved the blizzard that night to make it to the arena has inflated to thousands of (mostly-phony) claimants worldwide.

ARCHITECTS THROW A COSTUME BALL
January 23, 1931

At the 1931 Beaux-Arts Ball in New York, architects came dressed as the buildings they designed. Leonard Schultze showed up as the Waldorf Astoria, Ralph Walker as 1 Wall Street, and William Van Alen as the Chrysler Building, in a headpiece that spired dangerously four feet above his head and a cloak painted to look like the Chrysler's doors. (Ironically, doorways posed a real obstacle for him that night.)

Not all the guests at the ball were architectural royalty. Arthur J. Arwine, a Manhattan heating contractor, came dressed as a low-pressure heating boiler.

WINTER WONDERLAND
January 24, 1684

During the Great Frost of 1683–1684, the ice on the Thames River froze so thick that all of London came out to skate, sled, drink, and make merry.

A market sprung up offering food and beer, haircuts and souvenirs, and soon Londoners were racing horses and hackney coaches on the frozen waterway. The scene upon the Thames (dubbed "Freezeland Street" until it melted back into a river in the spring) was described on January 24, 1684, by one English chronicler as a landscape of "bull-baiting, horse and coach-races, puppet-plays and interludes, cooks and tippling," and other unspecified "lewd" activities.

The 1684 "Frost Fair" was the most celebrated of several such icy bacchanalias, which appeared in London semi-regularly during a 200-year period of global cooling known as the Little Ice Age. So dreamlike were these fairs that Londoners lost themselves in delirium. One 1683 report describes an enthusiastic skater gliding all the way out on the Thames toward the ocean, on his way to Belgium, before snapping from his wonderland reverie and turning back.

BABY DELIVERY
January 25, 1913

For a few years around the turn of the century, it was legal for parents in America to ship their kids through the mail. The first baby so delivered by post was James Beagle, an eight-month-old boy from Glen Este, Ohio, who arrived at his grandmother's doorstep on January 25, 1913, after a harrowing one-mile journey across town in a canvas mailbag.

Baby James weighed 10 3/4 pounds—just shy of the 11-pound limit for packages sent via Parcel Post (a service for handling heavier-than-average mail)—and his delivery cost his parents 15 cents in postage, which James wore in stamps on one side of his body. A newspaper assured readers that the "parcel" had been "well wrapped" and delivered safely.

A BIRD OF BAD MORAL CHARACTER
January 26, 1784

Shortly after America declared its independence from Britain, it adopted the bald eagle as its national bird. Until the day he died, Benjamin Franklin regretted the decision. In a letter to his daughter dated January 26, 1784, he wrote:

For my own part, I wish the bald eagle had not been chosen as the representative of our country. He is a bird of bad moral character; he does not get his living honestly. . . . Besides, he is a rank coward.

Franklin proposed an alternative:

The turkey is in comparison a much more respectable bird, and withal a true original native of America. . . . [He is] a bird of courage, and would not hesitate to attack a grenadier of the British guards, who should presume to invade his farmyard with a red coat on.

THOMAS CRAPPER DAY
January 27, 1910

According to a popular legend, the word *crap* comes from Thomas Crapper, the supposed inventor of the flush toilet. The story goes that Crapper's name was stamped on all his lavatorial devices, and when servicemen in World War I went to the latrine they would say, "I'm goin' to the crapper"—a word that gradually shortened to the colloquial profanity.

Logical as it sounds, it isn't true. In reality, *crap* comes from the Old French *crappe,* meaning *waste.* And though Crapper, an English plumber and engineer, *did* help develop the ballcock (the apparatus inside the toilet tank that allows the water to flush), he most definitely did *not* invent the flush toilet (that happened in 1596), and never had his name stamped on it. That story about WWI servicemen is just a load of you-know-what.

Nevertheless, every year on January 27, the anniversary of Crapper's death, people rejoice in a celebration of all things scatological. On Thomas Crapper Day 2007, an Arizona park ranger led a hike in Estrella Mountain Regional Park identifying different types of animal poop. On Crapper Day 2010, a New York coffee shop offered discounts to customers who donated a roll of toilet paper to charity. For a time, plumbers of distinction could even qualify for a special Crapper Day "Crapper Award," issued by the "Justice for Thomas Crapper Committee"—a now-defunct organization devoted to promoting Crapper's legacy, myth or not.

A SERENDIPITOUS DISCOVERY
January 28, 1754

On January 28, 1754, British nobleman and author Horace Walpole coined the word "serendipity" in a letter to his friend Horace Mann. Walpole used it in reference to the Persian fairy tale *The Three Princes of Serendip,* in which characters continually make pleasant discoveries by accident.

"Serendipity" was one of the few Walpole coinages that actually caught on. His other attempts at word creation—"muckibus" (the state of being drunkenly sentimental), "betweenity" (the state of being in between things), and "nincompoophood" (the state of being a nincompoop)—didn't make the cut.

WHALE OF A MESS
January 29, 2004

In January 2004, the largest animal ever recorded in Taiwan washed up on the island's western coast. Two weeks later, it exploded.

Researchers were taking the remains of the 56-foot-long, 60-ton sperm whale by truck to the National Cheng Kung University on January 29, 2004, when a buildup of internal gases caused the decaying carcass to burst apart. Blubber and guts splattered over the streets of Tainan, showering pedestrians and storefronts, and halting traffic while cleaners dealt with the mess. A rotting stink hung in the air for weeks.

Whale lovers with a taste for the dramatic can see the great leviathan on display—or what's left of its skeleton—at the Taijiang Cetacean Museum in Taiwan.

A POSTHUMOUS EXECUTION
January 30, 1661

In 1649, Oliver Cromwell helped abolish the British monarchy and overthrow King Charles I, but by 1660 the kingdom was restored and Charles's son was in power. Charles II now had it out for his father's foe. He accused Cromwell of treason and sentenced him to death. There was only one problem: Cromwell had died in 1658.

Not to be deprived of the satisfaction of killing his father's killer, Charles II exhumed Cromwell's corpse from Westminster Abbey on January 30, 1661, and had it publicly hanged, beheaded, and thrown into an unmarked pit. Oliver's head hung on a pike outside Westminster Hall for a quarter century, until a storm snapped the pole and it went crashing to the ground. From there, his noggin passed through the hands of apothecaries, businessmen, and private collectors, with a few stops at museums before finally receiving a proper reburial in Cambridge in 1960.

THE MOST DARING ROBBERY ON RECORD
January 31, 1874

Jesse James was known as much for his boasting as his banditry. On January 31, 1874, he and his gang of outlaws held up a train near Gads Hill, Missouri. After looting the safe and the pockets of several passengers, James handed the engineer a prewritten press release and instructed him to give it to the newspapers. He left a blank space to fill in the amount stolen. James's headline read: "The Most Daring Robbery on Record."

JACKIE AND JACKO
February 1, 1988

By the age of 46, Jacqueline Kennedy Onassis was twice widowed by two of the world's richest men, but she wasn't going to rest on her dowries the rest of her life. In 1977 the former First Lady took a part-time job as a book editor with Doubleday for a $20,000 salary, and resumed the working life she had long ago abandoned.

On February 1, 1988, Jackie's first major project hit bookstores, Michael Jackson's autobiography, *Moonwalk*. Jackie worked closely with Michael on the book for four years. Their pairing had seemed logical at first—two public figures leading notoriously private lives—but Michael's eccentricities soon overwhelmed Jackie. He missed deadlines, arrived late for meetings, and several times threatened to pull the plug when he didn't get his way. Some days Jackie had to hound him to read over her notes; other days he called her incessantly to complain about them. At one point Jackie confided to a friend, "Michael Jackson is driving me mad with his phone calls."

After the hardcover edition sold out its first print run, Jackson canceled the paperback edition, costing Doubleday potential millions. Jackie was no longer surprised or concerned. She had already moved on to other projects.

MONA LISA SMILE
February 2, 1987

Art historians have long debated the mystery behind Mona Lisa's smile—or if, in fact, she's smiling at all—but the subject of Leonardo da Vinci's 1503 painting didn't get her first medical diagnosis until 1987. According to a February 2 article in *Physician's Weekly,* Mona Lisa's smile is actually a symptom of Bell's palsy, a common nerve disorder caused by a weakening of the muscles on one side of the face. The condition would explain why Mona Lisa's left eye is narrower, and the left corner of her mouth higher, than the same features on the right. Dr. Kedar K. Adour, a leading ear, nose, and throat specialist quoted in the article, diagnosed the source as a swollen nerve behind the left ear.

THE BRIEF, WONDROUS LIFE
OF TULIPOMANIA
February 3, 1637

Ever since Europeans laid eyes on the tulip sometime in the mid-1500s, it has been the prize of nobility and royalty. But it wasn't until a rare virus broke out among Dutch tulips a century later, marbleizing them in swirls of vibrant color, that casual collectors became zealous connoisseurs. The rage swept down through Holland's middle classes, and by the 1630s the whole nation was mad for tulips.

Botanists began breeding for the prettiest patterns, merchants charged preposterous prices, and a new crop of flower painters captured their beauty in dazzling floralscapes. (Rembrandt has a classification of tulip named after him—the Rembrandt tulip—for his works during this period, although he was not known for painting tulips.) In one 1636 transaction, a single root of a *Viceroy* tulip sold for the following bill of items:

	Florins
Two lasts* of wheat	448
Four lasts of rye	558
Four fat oxen	480
Eight fat swine	240
Twelve fat sheep	120
Two Hogsheads of wine	70
Four tuns** of beer	32
Two tuns of butter	192
One thousand lbs. of cheese	120
A complete bed	100
A suit of clothes	80

A silver drinking cup	60
Total:	2,500
Modern equivalent:	$21,700

*1 last = 120 cubic feet of shipping space
**1 tun = 252 gallons

The trade reached such a frenzy by 1636 that merchants, impatient for the next harvest, began trading in off-season IOUs—promissory notes detailing the bulb in question and the date of its expected maturation. This airy exchange of promises formed a speculative bubble, and like all bubbles, it was bound ultimately to burst.

At a routine auction in Haarlem on February 3, 1637, buyers refused to bid on a rare tulip bulb. Almost overnight, tulips depreciated. The mania collapsed. Those who had sold off their stock while the fad was strong had made themselves extremely wealthy. Others had come out the other end paupers, possessors of a few worthless flowers they had bartered entire fortunes for.

DEATH KNELL
February 4, 1893

Before modern medicine, being buried alive was more than just an idle phobia. It actually happened. A lot.

Common procedure for dealing with an unconscious person was to hold a glass pane to his or her mouth. If the mirror stayed dry, the soul had departed. If it fogged up, there was life yet. But this primitive test was unreliable, prone to false positives and a diagnosis of death for comatose patients, who often awoke to find themselves in a box underground.

One concerned claustrophobe took up the cause. On February 4, 1893, Iowan inventor August Lindquist filed a patent for a "grave alarm," a bell on a string designed to help the interred alert passersby if they had been mistakenly buried alive.

Lindquist designed the string to run slack along the body, within easy reach of the corpse. He also outfitted the system with snorkel-like piping to funnel fresh air into the coffin, able to sustain the body until help arrived.

THE LONGEST WAR IN HISTORY
February 5, 1985

The first two Punic Wars both ended in prompt peace treaties, but the third took *just* a bit longer. On February 5, 1985, more than two thousand years after Rome waged the Third Punic War against Carthage in modern-day Tunisia (149–146 BCE), the mayors of the two cities finally signed a formal treaty calling it off. Technically, it's the longest war in history—though hostilities lasted only three years.

MOONSHOT
February 6, 1971

When NASA astronaut Alan Shepard went to the moon in 1971, he smuggled aboard two golf balls and a golf club head inside a utility pocket on his left thigh. On February 6, he set them on the lunar surface. The following is from the mission control transcript:

Shepard: Houston . . . you might recognize what I have in my hand as the handle for the contingency sample return. It just so happens to have a genuine six iron on the bottom of it. In my left hand, I have a little white pellet that's familiar to millions of Americans. I'll drop it down. . . . I'm going to try a little sand trap shot here. [Shepard lines up his shot and swings poorly.]

NASA: You got more dirt than ball that time.

Shepard: Got more dirt than ball. Here we go again. [He pushes the ball a few feet.]

NASA: That looked like a slice to me, Al.

Shepard: Here we go. Straight as a die. One more.

[Shepard finally connects, and the low lunar gravity carries the ball out toward the horizon.]

Shepard: Miles and miles and miles . . .

NASA: Very good, Al.

RESTORATION
February 7, 1845

William Lloyd, an alcoholic at the end of a weeklong bender, entered the British Museum on this day, and smashed the famous Portland Vase, a first-century Roman glass amphora. Due to an error in the wording of the law, Lloyd's attorney successfully argued that his client was only liable for destroying the glass case surrounding the vase, for which Lloyd was fined three pounds.

For the next 144 years, art restorers attempted to put the Portland Vase back together. A breakthrough occurred in 1948 when Bernard Ashmole, keeper of Roman antiquities at the British Museum, discovered thirty-seven forgotten fragments inside an unlabeled box and recognized them as the crucial missing pieces to the restoration. After several more rounds of reassembly between 1948 and 1989, the precious artifact was epoxied back together. Today, scarcely a crack can be detected.

JACK OF CLUBS
February 8, 1994

On this day, three-time Oscar-winner Jack Nicholson stopped at a red light in North Hollywood, selected a two-iron from his golf bag, and smashed it through the windshield of a fellow motorist in a fit of road rage. He was charged with vandalism and assault, and settled out of court for $500,000.

Nicholson later starred in the 2003 black comedy *Anger Management* as an anger therapist to Adam Sandler, a man who himself played a quick-to-rage golfer in the 1996 slapstick *Happy Gilmore*.

QUEEN OF BOHEMIA
February 9, 1893

Twenty-four-year-old Marie-Florentine Roger, an artist's model known around Paris as the "Queen of Bohemia," performed the world's first recorded striptease when she disrobed during a *tableau vivant* at the annual Four Arts Ball, at the Moulin Rouge, in Paris.

Roger was arrested for public indecency and fined 100 francs. Her arrest incited a massive student riot in defense of artistic freedom, during which students sieged Paris's Prefecture of Police. The army was called in and one protester was killed.

THE NAKED TRUTH
February 10, 1535

To protest the corruption of the Catholic Church, twelve Anabaptists ran naked through the streets of Amsterdam on February 10, 1535, in the first recorded instance of streaking as political protest.

The seven men and five women doffed and burned their clothing under order of Hendrik Hendriksz, a self-styled prophet who stirred his followers into a feverish excitement after seeing a child throw his slipper into a fire and deciding it was a sign from God to reject all bodily garments.

TOILET HUMOR
February 11, 1960

TV host Jack Paar risked his career for a joke. Here's the set-up:

An Englishwoman on a trip to Switzerland asks a local school-master for a recommendation on lodging. After he leaves, she realizes it doesn't have a bathroom. She writes to him asking if there is a shared "WC" ("water closet") anywhere in the area, but he interprets WC to mean "Wayside Chapel" and replies:

> *Dear Madam,*
>
> *I take great pleasure in informing you that the WC is situated nine miles from the house you occupy, in the center of a beautiful grove of pine trees surrounded by lovely grounds. It is capable of holding 229 people and it is open on Sunday and Thursday only. As there are a great number of people and they are expected during the summer months, I would suggest that you come early: although there is plenty of standing room as a rule. You will no doubt be glad to hear that a good number of people bring their lunch and make a day of it. . . . I would especially recommend that your ladyship go on Thursday when there is a musical accompaniment.*

After learning that NBC's censors cut the joke from his February 11, 1960, broadcast for its "indecent" subject matter, the host of *The Tonight Show* took a principled stand and quit his job on-air. "There must be a better way of making a living than this," Paar said, before storming off set.

Unfortunately, there wasn't. Paar swallowed his pride and came crawling back a month later. Upon his return, he strode confidently to his desk, looked straight into the camera, and said, "As I was saying, before I was interrupted . . ."

BREAKUP BARBIE
February 12, 2004

After 43 years of dating, Barbara "Barbie" Millicent Roberts finally ended her relationship with plastic boyfriend Ken Carson.

"It wasn't that they had some screaming fight or anything," said Russell Arons, Mattel's Vice President of Marketing. "But Barbie felt maybe, after 43 years, it was time." The publicity ploy backfired when Barbie and Ken fans called for a boycott of the toy company and circulated petitions to reunite their favorite plastic couple. After a seven-year effort, they were victorious. The pair got back together on Valentine's Day 2011. That afternoon, Barbie's Facebook page changed its status to "In a Relationship."

THE CASE OF THE PREHISTORIC SPARK PLUG
February 13, 1961

On this day, a group of geologists digging for gems in California found what appeared to be an ancient crystal geode. When they cut into the 500,000-year-old sediment, they found a small metal object, strangely modern in appearance, nested in a perfect circle of porcelain. The object turned out to be a 1920s-era spark plug—the kind used by Ford in his Model T.

The Coso artifact, as it's known, is a prime example of OOPArts, or "Out-of-Place Artifacts"—archeological anachronisms that confound our evolutionary timeline. There are many such relics: There's the London Hammer, a man-made iron tool found inside a 400-million-year-old rock; the Klerksdorp spheres, round, grooved objects tucked into 3-billion-year-old pyrophyllite deposits; and the Quimbaya airplanes, a collection of gold objects from the first millennium that resemble modern airplanes.

Very likely that Model T spark plug had slipped through a crack in the ground, rusted over, and melded with a much older rock, forming a natural concretion. That's the scientific hypothesis, at least. But if ever there was a field of study hijacked by pseudoscientists and conspiracy theorists, OOPArts is it. Some creative theories: the spark plug was left by a high-tech ancient civilization; it's a relic of a prehistoric visit to Earth by advanced extraterrestrials; it's detritus from a time travel mission to the past.

THE BELL TELEPHONE CONTROVERSY
February 14, 1876

Alexander Graham Bell and his rival, Elisha Gray, invented the telephone independently of each other and filed their patents on the exact same day, February 14, 1876. The patent examiner, Zenas Wilber, had served with Bell's lawyer in the Civil War and was heavily indebted to him for money loaned to cover his drinking habit. To absolve his debt, Wilber granted the patent to Bell instead of Gray.

Ten years later, Wilber had a pang of conscience and admitted his guilt in a sworn affidavit. He wrote:

> *[At that time] I was afflicted with and suffering from alcoholism, and [the patent's approval] was obtained from me when I was so suffering. . . . I am convinced that, by my action while Examiner of Patents, Elisha Gray was deprived of proper opportunity to establish his right to the invention of the telephone, and I now propose to tell how it was done.*
>
> *. . . I was in debt to [Bell's lawyer] Maj. Bailey at the time the application for Bell was filed in the office; in addition, I was under obligations to him for a present to my wife—a very handsome and expensive gold hunting case lady's watch. . . . I consequently felt under many and lasting obligations to him, and necessarily felt like requiting him in some degree at least by favoring him in his practice whenever and however I could.*

Alexander Graham Bell's legacy today is the result of an alcoholic's debt to his benefactor.

IMPERSONATOR
February 15, 1969

Vickie Jones, a 27-year-old aspiring singer, was arrested on February 15, 1969, for impersonating Aretha Franklin at a concert in Florida. When it came out that Vickie had been duped to perform by a dishonest concert promoter who promised her that she would sing *alongside* Aretha, not *as* her, Vickie became something of a celebrity herself. Shortly thereafter, another young singer in Virginia was booking shows pretending to be Vickie Jones.

ZEUS, PRESERVE THEE!
February 16, 600

When a person sneezed in Ancient Rome, the customary response would have been "May Jupiter preserve you." After a sneeze in Ancient Greece, the stricken would be enjoined to "Live! Zeus, preserve thee!" Sneezing was believed to expose the body to evil spirits, which could only be opposed by invoking a blessing from the divine—though exactly *which* divinity best dealt with sneeze-induced possession was a matter of dispute. On February 16, 600, Pope Gregory I finally put the issue to rest. As part of his crusade to expunge Europe of pagan influences, Gregory decreed that there is only one correct response to a sneeze—"God bless you."

KICK IN THE FACE
February 17, 1915

On this day, Bassett Digby, an esteemed British scientist, published the following Letter to the Editor in the London *Times*:

Sir,

A little light might be shed, with advantage, upon the high-handed methods of the Passport Department at the Foreign Office. On the form provided for the purpose, I described my face as "intelligent." Instead of finding this characterization entered, I have received a passport on which some official utterly unknown to me has taken it upon himself to call my face "oval."

Yours very truly,
Bassett Digby

DAIRY QUEEN
February 18, 1930

On the third day of the St. Louis International Air Exposition, Elm Farm Ollie, a two-year-old Guernsey from Bismarck, Missouri, became the first cow to fly in an airplane. During the flight she was milked, and her milk was sealed in paper cartons and parachuted over St. Louis. One carton reportedly ended up in the hands of another trailblazer of the skies, Charles Lindbergh.

Elm Farm Ollie's historic flight was honored in 1990 with an original operetta, *Madame Butterfat*, written by a Wisconsin lawyer-turned-food-hobbyist named Barry Levenson. Levenson (whose other eclectic accomplishments include founding the National Mustard Museum and heading the Criminal Appeals Unit of the Wisconsin Department of Justice) extols the rust-colored dairy cow in his feature song, "The Bovine Cantata in B-Flat Major":

Sing we praises of that moocow,
Airborne once and ever more,
Kindness, courage, butter, cream cheese,
These fine things we can't ignore.

CORNFLAKE WARS
February 19, 1906

Brothers John and Will Kellogg—creators of the Kellogg breakfast cereals—formulated their recipe for cornflakes in the Battle Creek Sanitarium, the health resort they ran together in Battle Creek, Michigan. Diet at Battle Creek was bland—mainly sugarless gruels, fiber-rich grains, and low-fat granolas. Like other religious conservatives of the time, the Kelloggs believed that a dull diet would reduce sexual excitability and "self-pollution." Cornflakes met these standards sufficiently.

The Kelloggs had no interest in selling their cereals—that is, until one of their patients, C. W. Post, stole the recipe for cornflakes from the sanitarium safe, added some sinful sugar to the recipe, renamed it "Post Toasties," and started Post Cereals. When Will saw the fortune that could be made, he too left the sanitarium for the cereal business. On February 19, 1906, he founded the Battle Creek Toasted Cornflake Company—later known as Kellogg's—and began purveying cornflakes to the millions.

SAME-DAY DELIVERY
February 20

Ralph Cummins is a Virginia football legend—a former star player at Emory & Henry College and the winningest high school coach in state history—but his greatest achievement occurred far away from the football field.

Ralph and his wife had their first child, Catherine, on February 20, 1952. Then came Carol, on February 20, 1953. Charles was next, on February 20, 1956; followed by Claudia on February 20, 1961; and finally little Cecilia on February 20, 1966. The Cummins clan is the only family in recorded history to produce five single children with the same birthdays. Guinness puts the odds of that happening at 17.7 billion to 1.

The coincident birthdays make sense when you consider the length of the high school football season. The running family joke is that Ralph wasn't so preoccupied in June once school let out. . . .

KILL SHOT
February 21, 1437

Tennis has the unusual distinction of contributing to the deaths of not one but two European monarchs. The first was King Louis X of France (he was actually history's first recorded tennis player): In 1316, he caught a chill after an exhausting game, developed pneumonia, and died. The second was King James I of Scotland: On February 21, 1437, while fleeing a mob of 30 assassins, James escaped through a sewer tunnel beneath his house only to find its exit blocked off. Days earlier, he had ordered his servants to seal the exit because he kept losing his tennis balls down there. His assassins caught up to him and stabbed him to death.

BIRTHSTONE
February 22, 10,000 B.C.

According to Hanna-Barbera, Pebbles Flintstone was born at the Bedrock Rockapedic Hospital at 8 p.m. on February 22, 10,000 B.C., weighing in at 6 pounds, 12 ounces. She premiered on TV on her 11,963rd birthday—in the February 22, 1963, *Flintstones* episode "The Blessed Event."

The question of Pebbles's birthdate is a favorite of TV game shows: It's been asked on both *Who Wants to Be a Millionaire?* and *Jeopardy!*

CAPONE THE MILKMAN
February 23, 1932

Chicago crime boss Al Capone made his fortune bootlegging liquor during Prohibition. But as Prohibition died out in the early 1930s, the man known to the world as Public Enemy No. 1 was staring unemployment in the face. Capone needed a legitimate business if he was to keep turning profits, and he found it ultimately in another popular beverage: milk.

With the structure for beverage distribution already in place, the dairy business seemed a natural transition for Capone. On February 23, 1932, with funds raised from the Chicago Milk Drivers Union (well, $50,000 in ransom for the return of their union president, whom Capone had his men kidnap), Capone purchased Meadowmoor Dairies and embarked on his new career in milk. It didn't last long. Within three months, Capone was sitting in prison for tax fraud.

Though his dairy career was short-lived, Capone *did* manage to leave his mark on one area of the industry. After one of his relatives became ill from drinking expired milk, Capone came up with the idea for the "sell by" expiration date, and lobbied to mandate it on all milk cartons.

CLEVELAND ROCKS
February 24, 1956

In an attempt to suppress rock and roll, the city of Cleveland, Ohio, barred all children under 18 from dancing in public without parental accompaniment. To enforce the ruling, Cleveland officials invoked a 1931 ordinance banning minors from businesses licensed to sell liquor—which covered most teenage dance halls, since they operated as bars on other days of the week.

Cleveland is now home to the Rock and Roll Hall of Fame.

THICKSKULLED
February 25, 1866

On this day, miners found a human skull buried beneath a million-year-old layer of lava, deep inside a mineshaft in Calaveras County, California. It made its way into the possession of Josiah Whitney, the State Geologist of California, who dated it to the early Pliocene Epoch (~5 million years ago). It was dubbed the "Calaveras Skull" and exhibited around the country as the world's first human.

Three years later, the *San Francisco Bulletin* reported that local pranksters had "got up the whole affair as a joke on Prof. Whitney"—having dug up a skull from a nearby graveyard and planting it in an ancient sedimentary layer for miners to find. In 1898, a Calaveras storeowner admitted, "The boys of those days were given to an inordinate love for 'joshing,' and, under the leadership of J. C. Scribiner, many practical jokes were perpetrated. Why, I had that skull, with the mate to it, in my store for weeks before the scheme of making sport out of it was thought of." Indeed, when scientists radiocarbon-dated the skull in 1992, they found it to be about a thousand years old—still pretty old, but not ancient.

Whitney refused to accept that he'd been pranked. He went to his grave as certain as ever that the Calaveras Skull was real.

SCAT GOT YOUR TONGUE
February 26, 1926

According to his own self-proclaimed legend, Louis Armstrong invented scat singing on February 26, 1926, when, midway through the recording of "Heebie Jeebies," he accidentally dropped his sheet music on the floor and began improvising nonsense words. Expecting the take to be thrown out, Louis threw inhibition to the wind and inadvertently coined a brand new vocal style.

NO-FLY ZONE
February 27, 1992

Still rattled by the paparazzo who parachuted into her wedding with a camera the previous October, Elizabeth Taylor took special precautions for her sixtieth birthday celebration: she had the Federal Aviation Administration clear airspace for a mile around the event and 1,000 feet above it. It's the only time a government has ever designated a no-fly zone for a birthday party.

DAY OF REST
February 28, 1643

Roger Scott, of Lynn, Massachusetts, was tried in court on February 28, 1643, for "common sleeping at the publick exercise on the Lord's Day"—that is, dozing at church on Sunday—"and for striking him that waked him." He was found guilty and whipped that December.

It was custom then, during church services, for a designee to go about the pews waking sleepers with a long stick. When he observed a slumbering man, he would rap him on the head; women he would brush lightly across the face.

LEAP YEAR PROPOSAL
February 29, 1288

Fed up with old-fashioned marriage customs, Scotland enacted a law in 1288 allowing a woman to propose marriage to a man— but only on leap days. The man was obliged to accept under penalty of fine:

It is statute and ordained that during the reign of her most blessed Majesty, for the yeare known as lepe yeare, the mayden ladye of bothe highe and lowe estate shall have liberte to bespeke ye man she likes, albeit he refuses to take her to be his lawful wyfe, he shall be [fined] in ye sum of one pound or less, as his estate may be; except . . . he can make it appeare that he is betrothed [to] another woman he then shall be free.

The penalty for declining a leap day proposal exempted no one. According to the 1606 British romance guide *Love, Courtship, and Matrimony*, even men of the cloth were bound by this curious convention:

The ladyes have the sole privilege during the time it continueth of making love, either by wordes or lookes, as to them it seemeth proper; and, moreover, no man will be entitled to benefit of clergy who doth in any wise treat her proposal with slight or contumely.

L'INVASION ERRONÉE
March 1, 2007

The strangest invasion in military history took place on March 1, 2007, when a company of 170 Swiss soldiers got lost and accidentally wandered into Liechtenstein.

Armed with rifles but no ammunition, the neutral Swiss marched more than a mile into foreign territory before admitting they'd made a wrong turn and heading back. "It was all so dark out there," said one disoriented soldier. To prevent hostilities, Switzerland called up Liechtenstein later that day to apologize.

WILD CARD
March 2, 1729

During a currency shortage in New France, in modern-day Canada, King Louis XV issued playing card money to replace coins. Like a standard casino deck, the cards were stamped with suits, numbers, and faces, but on the back they contained a note handwritten by the governor distinguishing them as legal tender. A card's denomination depended on how it was cut: if the card was fully intact, it was worth 24 livres; with its corners cut off, it counted for 12 livres. After the British conquered New France in 1760 and recirculated gold and silver coins, card money became nearly worthless. The French government offered Quebecois 25 percent of a card's value—6 livres to the full denomination, 3 livres to the half—to buy back the playing cards and take them out of circulation.

STICK UP
March 3, 1934

On this day, John Dillinger broke out of Crown Point jail using a fake pistol carved from wood, locking up 24 guards at timberpoint on his way out.

He fashioned the gun from a wooden washboard, a razor handle, and black shoe polish. After bluffing his way free, he stole an actual weapon—a Thompson submachine gun—using it to swipe the warden's car and speed away to Chicago.

Lillian Holley, the warden of Crown Point, suffered such embarrassment from letting Dillinger escape in broad daylight—and in her own car, no less—that she promised, "If I ever see John Dillinger, I'll shoot him dead with my own pistol." The Feds got to him first, killing him in Chicago later that year.

HOUSE OF NO CARDS
March 4, 1845

First Lady Sarah Childress Polk, a devout Presbyterian, moved into the White House on March 4, 1845, promptly banning liquor, card games, and dancing on the premises. For four years nobody (supposedly) drank a drop, laid a bet, or danced a step.

Ironically, it was Andrew Jackson who set up his friend James Polk with the sober and staid Sarah. Jackson was the U.S. presidency's biggest gambler and boozehound. Even as a young law student he was described as "the most roaring, rollicking, game-cocking, horse-racing, card-playing, mischievous fellow that ever lived in Salisbury." Needless to say, he didn't come around Sarah's sober White House much.

TRADING PLACES
March 5, 1973

Baseball has seen a lot of strange trades. There's Lefty Grove, the pitcher who was dealt to the Baltimore Orioles in 1920 in exchange for a new outfield fence. And Harry Chiti, the Cleveland Indians backup catcher who was traded in 1962 for a "player to be named later," which turned out to be . . . himself. The strangest trade of all, however, happened *off* the field between two teammates, New York Yankees pitchers Fritz Peterson and Mike Kekich. At a press conference on March 5, 1973, Peterson and Kekich announced that they had officially swapped families: Peterson was now living with Kekich's wife and kids, and Kekich had moved in with Peterson's wife and kids.

"Don't say this was wife-swapping, because it wasn't," Kekich told the press. "We didn't swap wives—we swapped *lives*." Kekich and the former Mrs. Peterson separated soon after, but Peterson and the former Mrs. Kekich went the distance. They are still married today.

FEATHERED FIENDS
March 6, 1890

The European starling is a major pest in North America today thanks to Eugene Schieffelin, a well-intentioned but misguided Shakespeare fan from Germany. On March 6, 1890, Schieffelin let loose 60 starlings into New York's Central Park in an attempt to introduce all of the birds mentioned in the works of Shakespeare to the United States. ("Nay, I'll have a starling shall be taught to speak nothing but 'Mortimer,'" says Hotspur in *Henry IV, Part 1*.)

The birds multiplied and now number more than 200 million in North America, where they wreak daily havoc in tree trunks (they steal nest holes made by other birds), on dairy farms (they steal grain feed meant for cows), and even at airports (they're prone to flying into plane engines). Agriculturists today consider the starling one of the costliest and most invasive species on the continent.

SMOKIN'
March 7, 1997

Ever since Portuguese traders brought tobacco to Asia in the early 16th century, Japan has smoked with gusto. But after a series of tough anti-smoking laws enacted in the mid-1990s, tobacco use plummeted. At the same time, lawsuits alleging secondhand exposure shot up.

The strangest charge from this period of litigious health consciousness was aimed at the Prime Minister himself. On March 7, 1997, a Japanese anti-smoking group filed suit against their chain-smoking head of state, Ryutaro Hashimoto, for making public remarks that encouraged citizens to light up. "Taxes on cigarettes are big revenue sources for the central and local governments," the two-pack-a-day premier had said during a trip to Singapore the previous January. "I will smoke as much as possible."

The lawsuit demanded 500,000 yen in damages sustained from Hashimoto's comments, as well as a court-enforced order that he quit smoking. The case was thrown out the following year.

OH, POPEYE!
March 8, 1939

On this day, Jack Mercer and Margie Hines—the cartoon voices of Popeye and Olive Oyl, respectively—wed at a private ceremony in Fort Lauderdale, Florida. For their first breakfast as a married couple they ate—what else?—spinach.

It wasn't the only romance forged in the voiceover studio. In 1991, the voice of Mickey Mouse (Wayne Allwine) married the voice of Minnie Mouse (Russi Taylor) in Hawaii.

ONE SMALL STEP FOR MANNEQUINS
March 9, 1961

On March 9, 1961, the Soviet Union launched a mannequin named Ivan Ivanovich into space aboard *Sputnik 9* to test radiation levels, pressure regulators, and communications equipment in preparation for Yuri Gagarin's orbital mission a month later. Ivan's "observations" about space were just a bit peculiar.

In programming Ivan's voice box (to test the craft's communications systems), the Soviets initially wanted him to recite technical details of the flight, but rejected the idea lest American intelligence intercept the messages and conclude Ivan was on a spy mission. They also opted not to play a recording of a man singing, for fear NASA radio monitors would think they'd stumbled upon an astronaut in the throes of space madness. At last, they decided on a transmission perplexing enough to shroud the nature of the test flight, yet not so obscure as to seem deliberately encrypted. During his orbit of Earth, Ivan at times broadcast choral music, and periodically recited a recipe for borscht.

DOOMSDAY RECONSIDERED
March 10, 1982

In *The Jupiter Effect* (1974), Cambridge-educated astrophysicists John Gribbin and Stephen Plagemann warn that a rare alignment of the planets on March 10, 1982, could set off a chain of cataclysmic events here on Earth, culminating in earthquakes and floods that could imperil human civilization. The book was a bestseller, and as the fateful date neared, many braced for the end of the world.

At the Gates Planetarium in Denver, switchboard operators fielded a deluge of panicked phone calls. "We've literally had people ask, 'Should I sell my house and move away?'" one employee said. Los Angeles residents, afraid of sliding into the void of the San Andreas Fault, fled the area for more tectonically stable ground. Meanwhile, a small Christian sect in the Philippines built a network of padded cubicles in preparation for the foretold Rapture.

Like all doomsday predictions before it, the Jupiter Effect failed to deliver. (To be fair, the tides that day *were* higher than normal—40 micrometers so, or about half the diameter of a human hair.) A year later, Gribbin and Plagemann published *The Jupiter Effect Reconsidered,* in which they explain why their prediction was off. It also became a bestseller.

THE SIMPLIFIED SPELLING MOVEMENT
March 11, 1906

Why does the *G* in *Margaret* sound different from the *G* in *margarine*? Why does *C* begin both *case* and *cease*? And why is it funny when a philologist faints, but not phunny to laf about it? English spelling is notoriously clumsy, with its surfeit of silent letters, fickle *i*'s before *e*'s, and cruelly innumerable variations on *there*. On March 11, 1906, a group of intellectuals—Mark Twain, Andrew Carnegie, and Henry Holt among them—founded the Simplified Spelling Board, an organization set on reforming English's thorny inconsistencies upon one simple motto: "Simplification by omission." That spring, the board submitted a list of 300 new spellings for immediate adoption. A sample appears below:

STANDARD SPELLING	SIMPLIFIED SPELLING
enough	enuf
through	thru
though	tho
bureau	buro
believe	beleve
caressed	carest
missed	mist

Theodore Roosevelt loved the new spellings. In August, he ordered the U.S. Government Printing Office to use them in all official documents issued by the executive department. Public reaction, however, was not so enthusiastic. Newspapers roundly mocked the Board's proposal, and in December 1906 the House of Representatives passed a resolution denouncing the new spellings and ensuring continued use of standard English orthography.

The simplified spelling movement never gained momentum and gradually fizzled over the next decade. But it would have a renaissance in an unlikely place: modern texting vernacular. With abridgements like *thru* and *tho*, textspeak follows the same omission-based maxim that governed the Simplified Spelling Board. Those wackadoo reformers—once the target of ridicule—had the last laf.

POOPED
March 12, 1993

Chief Mangosuthu Buthelezi wasn't the most popular member of the KwaZulu legislature. On this day, the South African leader detained his colleagues with a 400-page speech, which he recited slowly over the next 18 days. By the time he finished, the other legislators were too exhausted to challenge anything he'd said.

They took revenge 12 years later. In 2005, Buthelezi was taking his seat at the National Assembly when Minister Mosibudi Mangena, the leader of the Azanian People's Organisation, pointed at Buthelezi's feet. "Look! Look!" he cried. Beneath Buthelezi's chair was a small turd—an apparent gift from his fellow lawmakers. "I don't know what to make of it," Buthelezi said. "I'm just astounded that it should come to this in the holiest of holies."

MAALOX ERA
March 13, 2008

The afternoon before his 60th birthday, Billy Crystal fulfilled a lifelong dream: he joined the New York Yankees.

The comedian hatched the idea with Yankee shortstop Derek Jeter when they ran into each other at a Costa Rican resort. Jeter made the arrangements for Crystal to play in a spring training baseball game—a birthday gift for the aging comedian.

Crystal's dream wasn't quite what he expected. He struck out in his first at-bat and immediately announced his retirement. He later said that he was "the oldest person ever to play for the Yankees, and the first player ever to test positive for Maalox."

THE BOURNE AMNESIAC
March 14, 1887

On the morning of March 14, 1887, a Rhode Island preacher awoke with no idea where or who he was. After some stumbling interactions, he gathered that he had spent the past two months running a confectioner's shop outside of Philadelphia under the alias A. J. Brown. Psychologists diagnosed him with dissociative fugue, a form of amnesia in which a person forgets their identity and forms a new one, under which they might lead a perfectly normal life for a long period of time.

The man's real name was Ansel Bourne. He became the inspiration for the amnesiac character Jason Bourne in Robert Ludlum's novel *The Bourne Identity*.

BEWARE THE WEDDING MARCH
March 15, 1964

When asked why she married so often, Elizabeth Taylor replied, "I don't know, honey. It sure beats the hell out of me." On March 15, 1964, Taylor tied the knot for the fifth time (of eight), her first time (of two) to Richard Burton, one year after the scandal of their affair broke. They divorced in 1974, remarried in 1975, and divorced again in 1976. Fittingly, their last film together was the 1973 dud *Divorce His, Divorce Hers*, the story of the breakup of an 18-year marriage. Taylor said that if Burton hadn't died in 1984, they might have married a third time.

That Liz and Dick wed on the Ides of March was probably deliberate: they first hooked up on the set of *Cleopatra* (1963) after Liz's on-screen lover, Julius Caesar, is killed.

RED WEDDING
March 16, 453

As far as ill-fated unions go, Attila the Hun's final marriage (of probably dozens) takes the multitiered wedding cake. On March 16, 453, the ruler of the Huns married Ildico, a radiant young blonde of Germanic background. That night, he suffered a severe nosebleed and choked to death.

The Roman chronicler Marcellinus Comes suggested Attila was actually stabbed in his sleep by his wife. Most historians believe he drank himself silly and ruptured his esophagus.

UNITED STATES V. APPROXIMATELY 64,695 POUNDS OF SHARK FINS
March 17, 2008

In U.S. law, it's legal to ship shark fins—provided they're shipped with their corresponding carcasses. If a vessel has even one more fin than carcass, the entire shipment may be seized as contraband of the illegal shark fin trade. That's what happened in 2002, when the Coast Guard stopped and searched the *King Diamond II*, a U.S. vessel sailing through international waters off the coast of Guatemala, and found approximately 64,695 pounds of shark fins with no bodies attached. That kind of fin-to-carcass ratio just won't fly.

The seizure of the *King Diamond II* fell into a legal gray area: because the U.S. government didn't have jurisdiction over the owners of the boat, only the cargo itself could be charged. And so began the strange and wonderful U.S. Court of Appeals civil forfeiture case *United States v. Approximately 64,695 Pounds of Shark Fins*.

On March 17, 2008, after a year of debate and deliberation, the court ruled in favor of the shark fins.

EL FUSILADO
March 18, 1915

On March 18, 1915, Wenseslao Moguel, a Mexican revolutionary in Pancho Villa's army, was captured by federal troops and sentenced to death by firing squad. Moguel was shot nine times, including a mercy shot—the "coup de grace"—to the head at point-blank range to ensure death.

He took the bullets but survived: the next day, he crawled out from the pile of bodies and dragged himself to a local church, where he received medical treatment. Moguel went on to live another 60 years with half his face caved in, making frequent appearances on oddity shows like the *Ripley's Believe It or Not* radio program and Broadway's legendary "Odditorium" (which boasted "curioddities from 200 countries" and where fainting was fairly common). He even has a song written about him—"El Fusilado" ("The Executed One"), by the British band Chumbawamba.

FOOTBALL 101: DON'T FORGET THE BALL
March 19, 1892

One of the oldest rivalries in college football got off to a rather sluggish start. At the first Stanford–UC Berkeley game, played on this day at San Francisco's Haight Street Grounds, the teams were about to take the field when they realized Stanford's manager—a man by the name of Herbert Hoover, the future 31st President of the United States—forgot to bring the ball. The players waited an hour while a sporting goods owner in attendance departed on horseback to retrieve one from his shop.

MARCH 20 IN FAILED KIDNAPPINGS

WHEN: March 20, 1865
KIDNAPPER: John Wilkes Booth
TARGET: Abraham Lincoln

As the Civil War reached its final stages, Booth and six fellow Confederates plotted to kidnap President Lincoln and use him to bargain the surrender of the Union. On the day of the planned kidnapping, Booth assembled his associates on a road in Washington along Lincoln's expected route. The president changed his plans at the last minute to attend a reception at the National Hotel where, coincidentally, Booth was then residing.

WHEN: March 20, 1972
KIDNAPPER: Marlon Brando's ex-wife
TARGET: Marlon Brando's son

While Brando was abroad in France shooting *Last Tango in Paris,* his 13-year-old son Christian went missing. Brando hired a private investigator, the legendary Los Angeles P.I. Jay J. Armes, and on March 20, 1972, Armes tracked Christian to a cave in San Felipe, Mexico. After an investigation, Armes concluded that Brando's ex-wife, Anna Kashfi—with whom Brando had waged a years-long custody battle over Christian—had kidnapped their son from school in the U.S. several days earlier, drove him across the border, and offered a group of cave-dwelling hippies $10,000 to hide the boy from his father. Within days, Brando was granted sole custody of Christian.

WHEN: March 20, 1974
KIDNAPPER: Ian Ball
TARGET: Princess Anne of England

At 8 p.m. on March 20, 1974, as Princess Anne (the only daughter of Queen Elizabeth II) returned to Buckingham Palace following a charity event, her Rolls Royce was cut off by a white Ford Escort. The driver of the car, a man named Ian Ball, came out firing a pistol, hitting both Anne's bodyguard and chauffeur. Ball scooted in beside the princess and told her his plan to kidnap her. "Not bloody likely!" Anne replied, and she proceeded to have what she later called "a very irritating conversation" with the assailant. As she and Ball struggled in the backseat of the limousine, Ron Russell, a 6-foot, 4-inch former boxer, happened to be walking past. "He needs sorting," Russell recalled thinking. So he punched Ball in the back of the head with a solid right hook and led the princess to safety.

THE PAPIER-MÂCHÉ TIARA
March 21, 1800

On this day, Pope Pius VII was crowned at Venice in a papier-mâché tiara, a replacement for the one stolen by Napoleon during his overthrow of Pius's predecessor in 1798. Constructed from bits of paper and held together with glue, the new tiara was supposed to be temporary, but its light weight offered such a relief from the bejeweled monstrosity typically worn by His Holiness that it remained in the papal wardrobe for 45 years, passing from pope to pope like a family hand-me-down. Napoleon *did* donate a replacement crown to the papacy in 1804—but he deliberately made it too heavy (18.1 lbs.) to be worn comfortably.

THE MYSTERY AT LAND'S END
March 22, 2003

In the early hours of March 22, 2003, while transporting cargo from Cork, Ireland, to Lübeck, Germany, the *RMS Mülheim* ran aground at Land's End, a rocky headland on the west coast of England. By the afternoon, conspiracists were bubbling over with theories.

Like the Bermuda Triangle, Land's End, with its high incidence of shipwrecks, is a magnet for the superstitious. The coast is dotted with Stonehenge-like megaliths, Celtic shrines, and other ancient testaments to the region's mystique. In 1998, a team of Russian scientists added another layer to the lore when they identified the waters just off Land's End as the most likely location of the legendary lost city of Atlantis.

In reality, the cause of the *Mülheim* wreck was rather mundane. It turns out the chief officer, who was on watch at the time, had caught his pants on a control lever, fallen over, and knocked himself unconscious.

ONE THUMB DOWN
March 23, 1844

General Tom Thumb was a general in name only; the only battle the circus dwarf ever fought was with Queen Victoria's poodle. On March 23, 1844, the two-foot-tall Barnum circus performer was entertaining the queen at Buckingham Palace when, suddenly, her dog became excited by Tom's herky-jerky movements and started barking at him. Tom promptly drew his 10-inch sword—the linchpin in his mini soldier uniform—and engaged the poodle in combat. The queen and her guests laughed it up, assuming it was part of the show. To this day, it's unclear whether Tom was jesting for laughs or actually jousting for his life.

LONG SHOT
March 24, 1921

W. V. Meadows was 19 in the summer of 1863 when he was called up with the 37th Alabama Volunteer Infantry to defend the fortress city of Vicksburg, Mississippi, from a Union army attack.

On July 1, while sniping at Union soldiers through a hole in a sheet of boilerplate, Meadows took a bullet to the head and lost his right eye. At a Union hospital, surgeons probed in vain for the iron ball. Rather than risk a dangerous surgery, they left it lodged.

On March 24, 1921, Meadows, now 78, was sitting at his kitchen table in Alabama when he had a coughing fit. The Confederate veteran lurched forward and hacked violently. Out came the bullet that had been lodged in his head since 1863.

BACKDATED
March 25, 421

According to Italian tradition, the city of Venice was founded at the stroke of noon on Friday, March 25, 421, when a group of Paduan refugees gathered in the marshlands off the northern coast of Italy and laid the cornerstone of San Giacomo Church.

Venice's creation myth was part of a trend among early European chroniclers to attribute precise dates (and sometimes exact hours) to the births of cities based on little more than historical guesswork and clever religious correlating. (If a city's birth could be backdated to fall on a holy day, its creation would appear divinely ordained.) In Christianity, March 25 is the Feast of Annunciation—the day the archangel Gabriel whispered to the Virgin Mary that she would give birth to the Son of God.

According to other traditions: Rome was founded on April 21, 753 BCE (day of the pagan fertility festival Parilia); Baghdad on July 30, 762 (end of Ramadan); and Tenochtitlan on June 20, 1325 (summer solstice).

AN EROTIC LIFE
March 26, 1658

Samuel Pepys, England's first Secretary to the Admiralty, kept an erotic journal filled with juicy gossip—most of it about his own amorous affairs. Until he was 25, Pepys was cautious about sex; he suffered from bladder stones in his urinary tract that made those parts rather tender. On March 26, 1658, Pepys underwent surgery to remove an excruciating stone the size of a tennis ball, and he emerged a liberated man. The operation not only cleared his urinary tract, but a slip of the surgeon's blade also left him sterile. And so began an erotic life.

Pepys threw himself into the world with debaucherous abandon. He started up affairs with his secretaries, with his maids, with the daughters of friends, and dutifully recorded every detail in his journal. But no matter how much he indulged in carnal oblivion, Pepys never forgot that which had made it all possible. He had his bladder stone gilded, and he toasted it every March 26, the anniversary of his sexual liberation.

TO LIFE!
March 27, 1931

English novelist Arnold Bennett died trying to impress his girl-friend. When a Parisian waiter advised him against drinking the café's toxic tap water, Bennett took a sip to show his lady companion that he wasn't afraid of a little bacteria. *"Ah, ce n'est pas sage, Monsieur, ce n'est pas sage!"* the waiter protested—"Ah, this is not wise, sir, this is not wise!" Bennett developed typhoid and died on March 27, 1931, shortly after returning from Paris.

AND THE BAND PLAYED ON
March 28, 1984

After failed negotiations with Baltimore's mayor over stadium improvements, Baltimore Colts owner Bob Irsay covertly moved his entire NFL team to Indianapolis in the dead of night. The next morning, a city of passionately devoted fans awoke to find their team had gone.

The only part of the Colts remaining after the move was the marching band. They had been tipped off about Irsay's scheme and snuck into Colts headquarters to remove their equipment before the moving trucks arrived. They hid their uniforms in a cemetery mausoleum, and a few weeks later resurfaced as the now-independent Baltimore Colts Marching Band, retaining the name of their former team. The band played on for years in their home city, with no official organization to represent.

PINK AND BLUE
March 29, 1914

Fashion norms about gendered clothing have changed radically in the past century. Until the early 1900s, little boys in America regularly wore skirts and dresses, and modern color coordination—blue for boys, pink for girls—was virtually inverted. The first known reference to gender-specific hues appeared in the March 29, 1914, issue of *The Sunday Sentinel*. In a style tip that might befuddle the modern nursery fashionista, the author advises parents: "If you like the color note on the little one's garments, use pink for the boy and blue for the girl, if you are a follower of convention."

In 1918, the magazine *Earnshaw's Infants' Department* explained the logic of this pigmentary rule of thumb: "The generally accepted rule is pink for the boys, and blue for the girls. The reason is that pink, being a more decided and stronger color, is more suitable for the boy, while blue, which is more delicate and dainty, is prettier for the girl."

It wasn't until the post–World War II economic boom, when men resumed their role as the primary breadwinners and women as the primary homemakers (and shoppers), that manufacturers realized bright pinks and reds could drive more retail traffic—whether for shampoos, makeup, handbags, or clothing. At first a girlish fad, pink soon became a feminine norm as Marilyn Monroe, Jackie Kennedy, and other fashion icons of the 1960s were photographed in the wear. Finally, in the 1980s, with the availability of prenatal testing, the color association was cemented. Parents could now buy "girl" or "boy" merchandise ahead of their baby's birth, and retailers happily obliged with gender-colored diapers, strollers, bedspreads, bonnets, PJs, and play sets.

NOT ON THE RUG, MAN
March 30, 1998

Big celebrity interviews usually go to the big celebrity magazines—*People, Rolling Stone,* and the like—but niche magazines get some love too sometimes. On this day, *Floor Covering Weekly,* one of the world's leading magazines for the rug and carpet industry, published an interview with the Coen Brothers about their latest flick, *The Big Lebowski,* the story of a man seeking redress for a soiled rug.

"As an oriental design with a bull's eye/rosette in the middle with the rest of the rug radiating from it, the vibrant red Persian looks out of place in Jeff Bridges' house," explained the filmmakers-cum-rug-connoisseurs. "It fits the decor of the Pasadena mansion." It also tied the film together, man.

WILDCATS V. WILDCATS
March 31, 1997

In the 1996–'97 NCAA basketball season, the Kansas State Wildcats missed a playoff berth with a poor 10–17 record. At 7–22, the Northwestern Wildcats were just plain abysmal. The 24–10 Villanova Wildcats performed slightly better, but they collapsed in the second round of the playoffs.

The Kentucky Wildcats and the Arizona Wildcats fared best: they made it all the way to the final game at the RCA Dome in Indianapolis, where they faced each other for the championship on March 31. The Wildcats won.

EAT IT UP
April 1, 1957

On this day, Richard Dimbleby, the legendary BBC broadcaster, reported on the time-honored tradition of spaghetti farming in Switzerland:

> *The last two weeks of March are an anxious time for the spaghetti farmer. There's always the chance of a late frost, which, while not entirely ruining the crop, generally impairs the flavor, and makes it difficult for him to obtain top prices in world markets. But now these dangers are over, and the spaghetti harvest goes forward.*

The report ran along footage of a Swiss family picking long doughy strings from a grove of spaghetti trees near their home, and then laying them out to dry in the alpine sun. "Many people are often puzzled by the fact that spaghetti is produced at such uniform length," said the BBC newsman, "but this is the result of many years of patient endeavor by plant breeders, who've succeeded in producing the perfect spaghetti."

The next day, hundreds of aspirant spaghetti farmers phoned into the BBC asking how they, too, could begin growing their own spaghetti trees and harvesting plates of pasta direct from the source—a worthy return on one of the first large-scale April Fools' pranks ever pulled.

BACK TO WORK
April 2, 1996

After serving as President of Poland for five years, Lech Wałęsa resumed his old job as an electrician at the Gdansk shipyard, on the Baltic coast, repairing forklifts and electric vehicles for the equivalent of $1.40 an hour. When he returned to the shipyard gates on April 2, 1996, he was immediately handed a set of screwdrivers.

Wałęsa returned to his job for economic reasons: Poland does not provide pensions for its former presidents. "It just cannot be that a former president has no means of support," Wałęsa told reporters. "What is he supposed to do, become a barman or something?"

AUDIENCE OF ONE
April 3, 2017

Shia LaBeouf's *Man Down* didn't quite fire up the UK box office. In its opening weekend, the war thriller made just £7, the value of a single adult ticket sold at the Reel Cinema in Burnley, England. Only one person in all of Britain showed up to see it.

As soon as box office figures rolled in on Monday morning, Shia-bashing bloggers were back at their trade, trashing the embattled actor as an unsellable has-been. The negative attention seemed to have an energizing effect on ticket sales. By Tuesday, *Man Down* had tripled its opening weekend haul, selling an additional two tickets.

PACIFIST PILLOW FIGHT
April 4, 1968

Martin Luther King Jr. stayed true to his principles of nonviolence, for the most part. On April 4, 1968, the day of his assassination, King was in his room at the Lorraine Motel with Reverend Ralph Abernathy, preparing for a rally, when his friend and fellow activist Andrew Young walked in. King pretended to be angry with Young for not calling first. "He began to sort of playfully fuss with me," Young recalled. "He picked up a pillow and threw it at me. And I just threw it back. And all of a sudden everybody picked up pillows. And here we are—middle-aged men, almost—and we were having a pillow fight like children."

THE YEAR WITHOUT A SUMMER
April 5, 1815

So dense was the ash cloud produced by the April 5th, 1815 eruption of Mount Tambora, a volcano in Indonesia, that it blocked out the sun in parts of Europe and set off a geophysical chain reaction that disrupted the global climate for years.

During the next summer, snow fell in New York in June, Ireland suffered a devastating potato famine, and Western Europe darkened to the point that, in the words of Lord Byron, "the fowls went to roost at noon, and the candles were lighted as at midnight." Climatologists have a pet name for 1816: the Year Without a Summer.

The unusual conditions wound up shaping one of the world's most beloved horror tales. While confined to their Lake Geneva summerhouse for days due to the "wet, ungenial" weather, Mary Shelley and her companions—authors Percy Bysshe Shelley, John William Polidori, and Lord Byron—passed the time telling scary stories. Eighteen-year-old Mary concocted a darkly serious tale about a doctor and his hideous creation. She called it *Frankenstein.*

WORKING ON SHORTIES
April 6, 1907

Dr. James Naismith, the man who first nailed up a peach basket in a college gym and called it "Basket Ball," had a second, lesser-known invention to his name: a baby-stretching machine designed to make people taller, and thus better suited for the sport he created. On April 6, 1907, the *Lawrence Daily World* reported on Naismith's new contraption under the headline "Is Working on Shorties: Dr. Naismith Has Machine to Make People Taller":

> *The doctor has a device in his office by which he stretches his patients, and is at present working on these "shorts . . ." The experiment will be continued till the end of the school year. Doctor Naismith is willing to stretch anyone who desires it.*

The best time to stretch a future athlete, Naismith believed, was "from the age of 5 month to a year." During this stage of development, "the body is more or less elastic and that by a correct stretching system can be made to lengthen. It is claimed that by stretching the body thirty minutes a day for six months, it will lengthen two inches."

Naismith's one hesitation was not that his stretching device wouldn't work—he had no doubt that it would—but that it might work too well. The patient might grow too fast, he feared, to the point that there would be no way of stopping it.

SHAKY HANDS
April 7, 1926

On the morning of April 7, 1926, the Honorable Violet Gibson, daughter of Ireland's Lord Chancellor, left her convent in Rome with a Modèle 1892 revolver tucked into her right pocket. When she arrived at the Piazza del Campidoglio, Benito Mussolini was finishing up a speech to an assembly of Italian surgeons. She waited until he was done. Then she walked up to him, aimed her pistol a foot away from his face, and fired.

Mussolini's head jerked back. Blood trickled down his nose. When he looked up he saw Gibson cocking the hammer a second time. She fired again, but the pistol jammed.

The crowd fell upon the would-be assassin and pried away her gun while the Italian Premier was ushered to safety. After his wound was cleaned and dressed, he resumed his march on the Capitoline, dismissing the disruption as "a mere trifle." Gibson had come within an inch of killing Mussolini. In the end, she had merely grazed his nose.

It was Gibson's second failed attempt to take a life in less than a year. Ten months earlier, the shaky-handed (and then suicidal) gunslinger aimed a revolver at her own heart and pulled the trigger. She missed the mark that time, too, the bullet glancing off her rib cage.

GOODY TWO-SHOES
April 8, 1765

On this day, Irish author Oliver Goldsmith coined the phrase "goody two-shoes" in a fable about a poor girl who could only afford one shoe. Her luck changes when a charming gentleman proffers her a second shoe. Newly confident, with two covered feet, she goes on to live a life of charity, honesty, and goodliness.

Goldsmith was no goody two-shoes himself. Expelled from college for rioting, Goldsmith gambled himself into debt and lived off handouts from his uncle, Thomas Contarine. He died a pauper at 45 with, one imagines, only one shoe on.

THE CIVIL WAR FINDS
WILMER MCLEAN—AGAIN
April 9, 1865

Surrounded by Union soldiers in Appomattox, Confederate General Robert E. Lee sent a messenger into town to scout a place for a formal surrender. The messenger came upon the two-story home of local grocer Wilmer McLean. On April 9, 1865, Lee surrendered to Union General Ulysses S. Grant in McLean's parlor.

It wasn't the first time the war had turned up at McLean's doorstep. Four years earlier, McLean was living on Yorkshire Plantation, about 120 miles north of his future Appomattox residence. Through his property ran a small stream named Bull Run, and in July 1861 the first major battle of the Civil War broke out on McLean's farm—the Battle of Bull Run.

For years afterward, McLean boasted that the war began in his yard and ended in his parlor.

THE FAST AND THE FURIOUS
April 10, 1934

On this day, Clyde Barrow, of the bank-robbing duo Bonnie and Clyde, wrote a thank-you letter to Henry Ford for fashioning such a fine getaway car:

While I still have got breath in my lungs I will tell you what a dandy car you make. I have drove Fords exclusivly when I could get away with one. For sustained speed and freedom from trouble the Ford has got ever other car skinned and even if my business hasen't been strickly legal it don't hurt enything to tell you what a fine car you got in the V8.

Barrow was killed in his V8 a month later.

2 FAST 2 FURIOUS
April 11, 1866

Ulysses S. Grant's drive knew no bounds—or speed limits. On April 11, 1866, the U.S. Commanding General was arrested on the streets of Washington, D.C., for speeding in his horse carriage. Officer S. A. Bailey caught him kicking up dust in a residential neighborhood and, according to his police report, fined him five dollars for "fast driving."

Grant was arrested again that July for the same offense and fined another $5. A month after that, Grant seized the reins from his chauffeur in New York's Central Park and challenged an adjacent carriage to a race, which he won. (There were no officers around this time.)

Three years later, D.C. cop William West spotted a coach bounding recklessly down M Street. West ran after it, grabbed the bridle, and was dragged half a block before he brought it to a stop. He looked inside: it was Grant again. West apologized profusely to the newly inaugurated U.S. President, but insisted that his duty required him to impound the buggy. On the ride over to the police station, the officer confided that he, too, was an inveterate speedster, and had been arrested at least twenty-five times for driving too fast. The two became good friends.

FLIGHT COMPARISON
April 12

French aviator Pierre Prier piloted the first nonstop flight from London to Paris on April 12, 1911, covering a distance of 290 miles in 3 hours and 56 minutes. Exactly 50 years later, on April 12, 1961, Soviet cosmonaut Yuri Gagarin completed the first orbit of the earth, covering 25,000 miles in 1 hour and 45 minutes. Prier peaked at an altitude of about 200 feet. Gagarin topped out at 200 miles.

Both airmen were in their mid-20s when they made their groundbreaking flights, and both died shortly after during routine flight trainings: Gagarin in 1968, when his aircraft crashed near the town of Kirzhach, in Russia; Prier in August 1911, when his pupil shot him in the chest.

A WARNING
April 13, 1883

On this date, Alferd Packer, an American gold prospector on trial for cannibalizing several local politicians while snowbound in the mountains of Colorado, was found guilty of murder and sentenced to death. According to the next morning's newspaper, the presiding judge supposedly told him:

When yah came to Hinsdale County, there was siven Dimmycrats. But you, yah et five of em, goddam yah. I sintince yah t' be hanged by th' neck ontil yer dead, dead, dead, as a warnin' ag'in reducin' th' Dimmycratic populayshun of this county.

COLOR THERAPY
April 14, 1989

A study conducted by Yorkshire police, based on the research of Dr. Alexander Schauss, confirmed what psychologists and prison reformers had suspected for years: that pink jail cells have a calming effect on prisoners.

"Even if a person tries to be angry or aggressive in the presence of pink, he can't," explained Schauss, who pioneered inmate color therapy beginning in 1979. "The heart muscles can't race fast enough. It's a tranquilizing color that saps your energy. Even the color-blind are tranquilized by pink rooms."

Many correctional facilities have since adopted the rosy décor—much to the chagrin of inmates. When a prison in Switzerland went pink in 2013, inmates complained that it felt "like a little girl's bedroom." If the new Barbie-like boudoirs angered them, they had a hard time showing it.

LOOK OUT! LOOK OUT!
April 15, 1931

On this day, Plennie Lawrence Wingo, a failed restaurant owner from Abilene, Texas, began walking backward from Fort Worth to Istanbul, Turkey, decked out in a suit and a ten-gallon hat. He used a small rearview mirror mounted onto his eyeglasses to navigate, and on his back he wore a sign that read in large block letters, "Look Out! Look Out! Walking around the world backward!" He documented his adventures in the book *Around the World Backwards*.

CORRECTION
April 16, 1883

The following story appeared in the April 16, 1883, issue of the Kansas *Daily Commonwealth:*

> *About 2 o'clock this morning a ponderous meteor fell at the outskirts of the town, killing several head of cattle and completely destroying the dwelling house of Martinez Garcia, a Mexican herdsman, who, with his family, consisting of his wife and five children, are buried beneath the meteor. In its descent the meteor resembled a massive ball of fire, and the shock was similar to that of an earthquake. It is still hot and steaming. . . . The air was filled with sulfurous gas and the wildest confusion prevailed, as it was a long time before anybody could even conjecture what it was. This is the largest meteor that has ever fallen in Texas.*

In the days when newspapers still used aluminum press plates, it was often quicker to run a correction below an article than to have a typesetter fix the error and reset the whole plate. Beneath the meteor story, the *Commonwealth* ran this correction:

> *A dispatch from reliable gentlemen at Fort Worth, Texas, to the assistant press correspondent here, says that the story of the falling immense meteor at Williams' Ranche, Texas, last Friday night, is one of Joe Mulhatton's lies.*

TRUST ISSUES
April 17, 1790

At his death on April 17, 1790, Benjamin Franklin left a dowry of £2,000 to be split evenly by the cities of Boston and Philadelphia, with the stipulation that it not be touched for 200 years. By 1990, by the power of compound interest, the dowry had ballooned to $6.5 million.

The idea inspired one Jonathan Holden, a lawyer from New York, to make a similar bequest. In 1936, Holden distributed $2.8 million into a series of trusts—one to the Unitarian Church, another to Hartwick College in New York, a third to the state of Pennsylvania (in honor of Ben)—each with 500- or 1,000-year locks on them, with each one compounding annually. Once the trusts became payable in 2436 and 2936, they would be worth a striking amount.

So striking in fact, that it would wreak total havoc upon the world. At such a rate of growth, Holden's trusts would eventually overtake the global economy. By the twenty-fifth century, they would bankrupt the earth; by the turn of the millennium, they would out-value the known universe. The economy of 2936 would come crumbling down the day his trusts are released. Holden's dowry was a ticking time bomb.

In the interest of preventing economic Armageddon, a Pennsylvania judge voided Holden's compound rate in 1977. The trusts would be allowed to accrue *simple* interest, but the gains could not get rolled back into the principal. In 2936, therefore, Hartwick College will receive about $9 million—enough to fund a new lecture hall, maybe, but not enough to bankrupt the world.

THE GOOD OLD DAYS
April 18, 1930

It's easy to fall for the fallacy that things were better in the good old days (any historian will tell you the past was just as chaotic as the present), but in some cases our nostalgic longing for simpler times is perfectly justified. On April 18, 1930, a reporter for the BBC came on for his 8:45 radio bulletin, cleared his throat, and reported that . . . there was no news at all to report. He played piano music during the broadcast instead.

GO WEST
April 19, 1927

Mae West's first starring Broadway role was as a prostitute in *Sex,* a play that she wrote and directed herself. The show ran for 40 weeks before police raided it on grounds of obscenity. The cast was arrested, and West was put on trial.

Because prosecutors couldn't find a single line in the play that was actually obscene, the trial focused mainly on a belly dance performed by West. In one courtroom exchange, the arresting officer testified, "Miss West moved her navel up and down and from left to right." "Did you actually see her navel?" West's attorney asked. "No," said the cop, "but I saw something in her middle that moved from east to west." The gallery snickered.

On April 19, 1927, West was sentenced to 10 days in prison for "corrupting the morals of youth." Somehow she charmed herself down to eight: the warden released her two days early for good behavior. West later said it was "the first time I ever got anything for good behavior."

BUNNY BUGS OUT
April 20, 1979

On this day, U.S. President Jimmy Carter was fishing in the swamps of Plains, Georgia, when a large white rabbit swam toward his canoe, hissing and gnashing its teeth. Carter splashed the water with his paddle and the animal swam away. The day continued without further incident.

A few months later, Carter's press secretary mentioned the banal encounter to a journalist, who seized it and blew it up into a tale about a "killer" rabbit that tried to attack the president. Carter's swamp squabble became front-page news, and late-night comics skewered the president endlessly. The final hammer fell with *The Washington Post*'s front-page story "Bunny Goes Bugs: Rabbit Attacks President," which featured a *Jaws* parody illustration under the all-caps header "PAWS."

The killer rabbit incident became one of the most memorable events of Carter's presidency. Some say it cost him the 1980 election.

IN SYNC
April 21, 1910

In 1909, Mark Twain made a bold prediction about his death:

> *I came in with Halley's Comet in 1835. It is coming again next year, and I expect to go out with it. It will be the greatest disappointment of my life if I don't go out with Halley's Comet. The Almighty has said, no doubt: "Now here are these two unaccountable freaks; they came in together, they must go out together."*

The cycle of Halley's Comet is approximately 75 years. It was visible in the sky when Twain was born in November 1835. It was visible again the day he died, April 21, 1910.

The freaks were indeed in sync.

WRESTLER-IN-CHIEF
April 22, 1832

Before he became President of the United States, Abraham Lincoln was a champion youth wrestler. He won his county title as a teenager in Indiana, and racked up nearly 300 victories in all before giving up the sport for a political career in 1832. In fact, in 12 years of amateur wrestling, Abe pinned every single one of his opponents but one.

The date was April 22, 1832. Twenty-three-year-old Abe had enlisted a day earlier as a volunteer militiaman in the Black Hawk War. When his company arrived at its encampment in Beardstown, Illinois, a dispute arose with another unit over their claim to the same spot. Lincoln offered to wrestle for it. He was pitted against 25-year-old Lorenzo Dow Thompson, a top-ranking amateur wrestler from Union County. The company men formed a ring as the wrestlers locked arms and began grappling.

"We Sangamon county boys believed Mr. Lincoln could throw any one," recalled one of Lincoln's military comrades, "and the Union county boys knew no one could throw Thompson. So we staked all slick and well-worn quarters and empty bottles on the wrestle."

Young Lincoln had earned a reputation back home for his strength after winning a wrestling match against Jack Armstrong, the leader of a group of bullies known as the "Clary's Grove Boys," and he hoped to establish the same rep on his first day in the military. (The future president was also notorious as a trash-talker: He once bellowed to a rowdy crowd after pinning his opponent, "I'm the big buck of this lick. If any of you want to try it, come on and whet your horns.") But his competitor was stronger and quicker than he expected. Thompson threw the 6-foot, 4-inch future president to the ground on the first hold.

Lincoln got up, brushed himself off, and was promptly taken down again. After the second time, Lincoln accepted defeat—the first and only loss of his career. "Boys," said Lincoln to his backers, "give up your bet."

Lincoln retired from wrestling shortly after, drawn away by the prospect of a political career. He is now enshrined in the National Wrestling Hall of Fame.

LIFETIME ACHIEVEMENT
April 23, 1374

In gratitude for his literary contributions, King Edward III granted Geoffrey Chaucer a gallon of wine daily for life—sort of a lifetime achievement award. The *Canterbury Tales* author collected his liquid pension until Edward's death in 1377, at which time Ed's successor commuted it to a monetary grant of 20 marks a year.

MISATTRIBUTION
April 24, 1980

On this day, University of Chicago statistics professor Stephen Stigler published "Stigler's Law of Eponymy," which states that "no scientific discovery is named after its original discoverer." Examples of Stigler's Law include: The Pythagorean theorem (already known to Babylonians before Pythagoras); Halley's Comet (spotted by the Chinese two millennia before Edmond Halley); and the Venn diagram (introduced by Leonhard Euler a century before John Venn).

Even Stigler's Law is an example of Stigler's Law: It was first proposed in 1968 by a sociologist named Robert Merton.

NOT SO FAST
April 25, 1792

When the guillotine was introduced in France in 1792, the French lower classes railed against it—not because it was inhumane, but because it wasn't inhumane *enough*. The first man to lay his neck on the contraption was Nicolas Jacques Pelletier, a highwayman convicted of robbery in the rue Bourbon-Villeneuve in Paris. Crowds gathered on April 25, 1792, for Pelletier's execution but were disappointed when the display ended in a swift, precise chop. Lacking the long agony of the breaking wheel or the violent convulsions of the noose—both of which ensured maximum degradation for the victim, and a darn good show for the audience—the new apparatus was quick and painless, comparatively kind. The people voiced their verdict at once: as they dispersed from the site, they started up a rousing chant of "Bring back our wooden gallows!"

SPECIAL EXCEPTION
April 26, 1569

In the sixteenth century, Englanders were prohibited from playing sports on Sunday, with the exception of a single chicken merchant in Middlesex named John Seconton Powlter.

On April 26, 1569, Queen Elizabeth I granted a special license to Powlter, who, "having four small children, and fallen into decay" would henceforth be allowed "to have and use some plays and games at or upon several Sundays, for his better relief, comfort and sustentation."

Sports that only John was allowed to play included:

The shooting with the standard, the shooting with the broad arrow, the shooting at twelve score prick, the shooting at the Turk, the leaping for men, the running for men, the wrestling, the throwing of the sledge, and the pitching of the bar, with all such other games as have at any time heretofore or now be licensed, used, or played.

In 1618, Elizabeth's successor James I published the *Book of Sports,* a declaration allowing Sunday sporting throughout England.

MILKING MILTON
April 27, 1667

By the time John Milton published *Paradise Lost* in 1667, he'd been blind for 15 years. Every night he wrote a few dozen lines in his head, and in the morning he recited them to a transcriber—a process he fondly referred to as being "milked." Milton's daily milking carried on for a decade. During that time he buried two wives and served a prison sentence at the hands of Charles II. Blind, alone, and desperate for money, Milton hastily sold the copyright to *Paradise Lost* on April 27, 1667, for a mere five pounds. When the first printing sold out, he earned five more. Ten pounds was all that the English poet ever earned for his masterwork.

REEFER MADNESS
April 28, 1192

On this day, the King of Jerusalem was killed by the Hashashin, a secret order of professional murderers who carried out targeted slayings under command of their leader, Hassan ibn al Sabbah. They are better known by their Anglicized name: *Assassins*.

When Marco Polo retold the story of the Hashashin to his fellow Venetians, he inadvertently spread a false rumor he'd picked up in the Orient: that the Hashashin smoked *hashish* as part of their military training—which was supposedly how they got their name. Soon, the gossip in Europe was that a violent group of hashish addicts was going around Persia assassinating people willy-nilly.

The story got further corrupted in the 1930s when Harry J. Anslinger, head of the Federal Bureau of Narcotics, worked the Hashashin into his anti-marijuana propaganda by branding the secret society as an ancient example of reefer madness.

KILL THE SQUIRRELS
April 29, 1918

In 1918, America found itself entangled in two wars: one with the great and powerful German Empire, and the other with a small and unassuming rodent. The California ground squirrel (the less bushy cousin of the tree squirrel) was costing the state $30 million in ravaged crops every year—money that might better serve the war effort overseas. So in defense of global liberty, California declared April 29 the start of "Squirrel Week," and dedicated seven days to wiping out the little critters.

Rather than hire trained exterminators for the job, California horticulture commissioner George H. Hecke enlisted schoolchildren. "Dear boys and girls," began a recruiting pamphlet, "Is there one of your number who would like to be a member of a company made up of American boys and girls fighting to protect your big brother or cousin at the front in Europe?"

The pamphlet encouraged kids to "organize a company of soldiers in your class or in your school, march them out where the squirrel army is eating the food that should go to your brothers and cousins, and win your battle." Hecke offered cash prizes—$50 for first place, $30 for second, $20 for third—to the those who could slaughter the most squirrels in a week.

By the end of Squirrel Week, American tykes had slain more than 100,000 rodents—most either shot with pellets or poisoned with Hecke's special barley poison. (A recipe was included in the pamphlet.) Misjudging the scale of the carnage, Hecke had asked his child army to sever the slaughtered squirrels' tails and mail them to his office for tallying. Before the week was out, the *Sacramento Union* reported a "pronounced odor which has begun to permeate the offices of the state horticultural commission as a result of the accumulation of ground squirrel tails."

THE SPY WHO DUPED ME
April 30, 1943

The most daring spy operation of modern times has to be Operation *Mincemeat*—if only, for the fact that its chief agent, William Martin, was dead when it took place. The scheme involved plucking a fresh corpse from a London morgue and outfitting it with a British uniform, military medals, love letters, a life jacket, photos of a fake girlfriend, falsified pilot credentials, and "top secret" documents detailing an Allied invasion of Greece—kind of a Trojan gift to the Axis loaded with misleading intelligence. "Major William Martin," as he was identified in his papers, was then set afloat near the southern coast of Spain, where the tide would presumably bring him into the hands of Nazi-sympathizers.

On the morning of April 30, 1943, a local sardine fisherman casting out near the small village of Punta Umbria spotted Martin's body and alerted Spanish authorities. They informed a naval judge, who in turn told the Vice-Consul, and thus the news ran up Spain's pro-Axis chain to Hitler's circle. While Joseph Goebbels, the Nazi Minister of Propaganda, doubted the documents' authenticity, Hitler believed them to be real, so he ordered Nazi troops to Greece to block the supposed invasion. The Allies, meanwhile, stormed defenseless Sicily instead, and from that moment Hitler was on the defensive. The Axis would never recover.

If this spy thriller seems straight from the mind of Ian Fleming, that's because it was. The creator of James Bond was a lieutenant commander in the British Naval Intelligence during World War II and authored the 1939 "Trout Memo," which first laid out the plan of using a faked drowned body to feed the Axis false military intelligence.

TAKE IT TO THE BANK
May 1, 1932

In the 1930s, banks in Siam regularly employed monkeys to test counterfeit coins. When the coins arrived at the bank, the teller would pass them along to a monkey assistant who would bite down on each one to determine its quality. (Tooth marks indicated a fake.) The May 1, 1932, *Brooklyn Daily Eagle* reported on this strange practice:

> *Most of the larger banks in Siam have one or two monkeys behind the counter to help the cashier. One cashier told me his monkey assistant handled thousands of pounds' worth of coins of all descriptions every month, and he had never yet known it to make a single mistake in "spotting" bad coins.*

These simian assistants were kept on the bank's payroll, and from their wages the cost of bananas and other foodstuffs was deducted. "They are housed in quarters of their own on the bank premises," the article went on, "and every means is taken to allow them sufficient liberty after their day's work is over."

SOB SISTER
May 2, 1904

Crooner Bing Crosby always insisted his date of birth was May 2, 1904. He was actually born on May 3, 1903. The switch occurred when Bing was a child: His little sister, Mary Rose, also had a May 3 birthday, and in a fit of sibling indignation demanded that she have the date all to herself. Their father obliged and assigned Bing a new birthday—though why he shaved off an extra year is unclear.

THE ENDS OF THE EARTH
May 3, 7138

According to the Mayan Long Count calendar—or, rather, according to a modern cultish interpretation of it—the world should have ended on December 21, 2012. But doomsayers, worry not; we still have May 3, 7138, to look forward to. That, in the Mayan timekeeping system, is the *next* day the world is going to end.

BACK FROM THE DEAD
May 4, 1891

On this fictional day in Sir Arthur Conan Doyle's story "The Final Problem," Sherlock Holmes plummeted to his death off Reichenbach Falls in Switzerland.

Reader responses spanned from grief (fans took to the streets wearing black armbands) to denial ("Keep Holmes Alive" clubs circulated petitions to reverse Sherlock's death) to anger (one woman stalked Sir Arthur down a London street and thumped him with her umbrella). *Strand Magazine,* which published the Holmes stories, lost 20 thousand subscribers and received sack loads of hate mail, as though with a little editorial fudging the periodical could have kept Holmes alive.

Eight years later, Sherlock did come back to life. Doyle revived the detective—partly due to public pressure, partly because of a dwindling bankroll—for an *interquel* (a story that takes place between the original and the sequel) set before Holmes's death. The following year, Doyle caved completely. In "The Adventure of the Empty House" (1903), he reveals that Sherlock never died at all; his death was merely faked to throw off his nemesis, Professor Moriarty. Doyle's nifty act of retroactive twistery allowed him to continue spinning out Sherlock stories until his own death in 1930.

LAST WISHES
May 5, 1821

Upon his death, in accordance with his last wishes, Napoleon Bonaparte's head was shaved and his hair divided among his closest friends. A recent analysis of the emperor's chestnut locks turned up high levels of arsenic—more than 10 times the normal amount—suggesting that his "natural" death may not have been so natural after all—nor his "friends," perhaps, so friendly.

IGNITE *TONIGHT*
May 6, 1994

During an appearance on *The Tonight Show with Jay Leno,* comedian-provocateur Bobcat Goldthwait doused his chair in lighter fluid and set it ablaze with a barbecue lighter that he'd hidden up his sleeve. Leno came to the rescue with a splash of coffee, but not before the chair took a good charring. Goldthwait was fined $3,398 ($2,700 for arson, $698 for a new chair) and ordered to tape a public service announcement about fire safety.

The stunt came during a period when Goldthwait was trashing television shows left and right. A few days before his stunt on Leno, he appeared on *The Arsenio Hall Show* to protest its cancelation by Paramount Studios. Goldthwait showed up with spray-paint and wrote "Paramount Sucks" on the stage backdrop, hurled furniture cushions into the audience, and put his boot through a television monitor. Arsenio had to wrestle his unruly guest to the ground.

WHAT IS LOVE?
May 7, 1922

Forced to rule on whether a man named William Laub really loved a woman named Beatrice Buber—or whether he had made false pretenses to obtain $1,100 from her—a San Francisco judge found himself poetically confounded:

How can a court determine whether or not he loved her? Love is a most puzzling thing. It is an intangible something— here, then there, and then gone.

To be sure, some persons pretend they are in love when they are not, and maybe it was so with Laub. But how can the court judge? In the next place, what is love? Oh, well, the case is dismissed.

JUMPER
May 8, 1885

In a failed suicide attempt, Sarah Ann Henley, a barmaid from Bristol, England, jumped from the Clifton Suspension Bridge only to have her skirt billow with an updraft and parachute her safely onto a muddy bank.

"The rash act was the result of a lovers quarrel," reported the *Bristol Magpie.* "She, in a state of despair, rushed to end her life by the fearful leap from the Suspension Bridge. There being a slight breeze blowing on Friday, the young woman's clothes were inflated and her descent was thereby considerably checked."

Two passersby found Henley in the thick, low tide sludge along the River Avon, 245 feet below her drop point, and escorted her to a nearby railway station where a doctor attended to her. The story of her miraculous survival spread and proposals of marriage flooded in. She never went back to the lover who scorned her.

LITERARY PROPHET
May 9, 1898

Morgan Robertson accurately predicted not one but *two* iconic naval disasters. On May 9, 1898, the author and seaman published *Futility,* a novella about a fictional luxury ocean liner named the SS *Titan.* One cold mid-April night, the *Titan* strikes an iceberg in the North Atlantic and sinks to the bottom of the ocean, 400 miles off the coast of Newfoundland. Fourteen years later, on a cold mid-April night, the *Titanic* struck an iceberg in the North Atlantic and sank to the bottom of the ocean, 400 miles off the coast of Newfoundland.

After the *Titanic* disaster, Robertson acquired a reputation as something of a novelist-prophet—a writer through whom the future spoke its secrets. He soon confirmed his reputation. Two years later, Robertson published "Beyond the Spectrum" (1914), a short story about a Japanese sneak attack on Hawaii.

FRUIT OR VEGETABLE?
May 10, 1893

Botanically speaking, a tomato is a fruit. Legally speaking, it's a vegetable. The debate was settled on this day in the 1893 U.S. Supreme Court case *Nix v. Hedden,* a suit brought by New York grocer John Nix against the Collector of the Port of New York, Edward Hedden, to recover taxes levied upon his tomato imports. For years, Hedden had been taxing Nix's tomatoes as vegetables, which were subject to a 10-percent import duty. Nix knew tomatoes to be fruits, which U.S. law allowed to be imported tax-free.

Because of its internal seed structure, a tomato *is* a fruit. But the court didn't see it that way. In his decision, Justice Horace Gray argued that despite their technical classification tomatoes are traditionally served "at dinner in, with, or after the soup, fish, or meats which constitute the principal part of the repast, and not, like fruits generally, as dessert." (Culinarily, they are closer to carrots than peaches, you could say.)

The Supreme Court ruled in favor of Hedden: tomatoes are vegetables, not fruits, and should be taxed accordingly.

THE POPGUN PLOT
May 11, 1795

Dr. James Parkinson, the man for whom "Parkinson's disease" is named, was part of a secret radical society that once tried to assassinate King George III with a poison dart. When the "Popgun Plot" failed, four of Parkinson's closest radical friends were arrested for treason. On May 11, 1795, Parkinson testified in their support before the Queen's Privy Council.

Thanks in part to his testimony, the alleged assassins were acquitted, but Parkinson's brush with the law deterred him from a life of political radicalism. He turned instead to another interest: medicine. In 1817, he published "An Essay on the Shaking Palsy," which doctors still use to diagnose Parkinson's disease today.

POPULAR DISBELIEF
May 12, 1593

On this day, the Queen's Privy Council searched the chambers of Thomas Kyd, the English playwright whose *Spanish Tragedy* inspired Shakespeare's *Hamlet,* and found in his possession "vile heretical conceits denying the eternal deity of Jesus Christ."

Kyd claimed that the papers belonged to his roommate, playwright Christopher Marlowe. Police arrested Marlowe on May 20 for the crime of atheism, and a week later he was found stabbed to death in South London. Investigators later uncovered documents proving that Marlowe had been a spy for the Crown, and may have been framed by the Privy Council for fear he would out several members as atheists.

PORT SHEEP
May 13, 1604

On May 13, 1604, French explorers Pierre Dugua de Mons and Samuel de Champlain landed at Nova Scotia, Canada, to scout locations for a permanent French colony. A sheep, excited by the sight of land after the long voyage, jumped overboard some distance from shore and nearly drowned. The crew rescued the sheep and then ate it. Mons named the landing spot Port Mouton, after the French word for *sheep*. In English, it is Port Mutton.

BARE LEGS FOR PATRIOTISM
May 14, 1942

On this day, Britain introduced its "Bare Legs for Patriotism" campaign, an appeal to women to ration their nylons so the material could be fashioned into parachutes, ropes, and other war supplies.

A new trend emerged from this austerity measure: "liquid stockings." Using a foundation brush, British women would paint a nude cream onto their legs to create the illusion of hosiery. "Leg Lotion gives the glamorous effect of super-sheer stockings, out-flatters your finest nylons!" read a 1940s advertisement. "It goes on like a dream. And it magically makes your legs look slimmer." For the full effect, women would draw a perfect stocking "seam" up the back of the leg using an eyeliner pencil.

The broader "beautility" campaign of British austerity measures was said to have saved the country £600 million by 1943.

GRACE AND A CODPIECE
May 15, 1602

On this day, English seaman Bartholomew Gosnold "discovered" (in the colonialist sense of the word) Cape Cod while searching the coast for sassafras, a root that commanded a high price in London as a purported cure for syphilis.

Gosnold sensibly named his landing site after the region's other major commodity, cod—though, at the time, this might have elicited some giggles as well. As any student of Shakespeare will tell you, "cod" was Elizabethan slang for male genitalia.

CAN'T STAND THE HEAT
May 16, 1830

French physicist Joseph Fourier was one of the nineteenth century's foremost experts on thermodynamics. He is best known for his discovery of the "greenhouse effect"—the process by which Earth insulates heat and warms itself. In his later years, Fourier became convinced of the supposed healing powers of heat, and he took to overheating his house and wrapping himself up tightly in blankets as a daily health regimen. In this swaddled state Fourier tripped down the stairs and died on May 16, 1830.

A MONSTROUS CARBUNCLE
May 17, 1984

For a man with zero architectural training, Prince Charles had some strong opinions on building design. On May 17, 1984, the Prince of Wales trashed a proposed extension of the National Gallery in London, calling it a "monstrous carbuncle on the face of a much-loved and elegant friend." In the same speech, Charles criticized plans to build a skyscraper to replace the Victorian Mappin & Webb building, and when plans for that were later scrapped, he said its replacement looked "rather like an old 1930s wireless [radio]."

In 1987, Prince Charles said of the new Canary Wharf Tower: "I personally would go mad if I had to work in a place like that."

In 1988, Charles said the Birmingham Central Library designed by John Madin looked like "a place where books are incinerated, not kept."

In 2008, he described a university lecture hall as looking "like a dustbin."

Lord Palumbo, the chairman of the British Arts Council, said of Charles, "I can only say God bless the Prince of Wales, and God save us from his architectural judgment."

REIGNING CHAMPS
May 18, 1924

The U.S. rugby team arrived at the 1924 Paris Olympics at the peak of French anti-Americanism. When their ship pulled into Boulogne, the Americans were held in port for hours while immigration officials deliberately dallied with their visas. When they arrived at the Olympic practice fields, they found that security had barred their access. When the Americans scaled the fence of Colombes Stadium to scrimmage on the championship field instead, the French stole the team's equipment out of their dressing room and hid it.

Hostilities came to a head on May 18, 1924, at the championship game between the United States and France. Fifty thousand fans showed up to Colombes Stadium to jeer their Yankee foes. When the United States pulled out a miraculous 17–3 win, drunken spectators tossed bottles and rocks onto the field, scuffles broke out in the stands, and one fan knocked an American reserve player unconscious with a walking stick.

The Olympic Committee promptly banned rugby from all future Summer Games. The United States remained the reigning Olympic rugby champion for 92 years, until the sport was reinstated for the 2016 Summer Games in Rio.

FART PROUDLY
May 19, 1780

In response to a call for scientific papers from the Royal Academy, Benjamin Franklin submitted a tongue-in-cheek essay proposing that scientific research be directed toward improving the odor of flatulence:

> *It is universally well known, That in digesting our common Food, there is created or produced in the Bowels of human Creatures, a great Quantity of Wind. That the permitting this Air to escape and mix with the Atmosphere, is usually offensive to the Company, from the fetid Smell that accompanies it. That all well-bred People therefore, to avoid giving such Offence, forcibly restrain the Efforts of Nature to discharge that Wind . . . Were it not for the odiously offensive Smell accompanying such Escapes, polite People would probably be under no more Restraint in discharging such Wind in Company, than they are in spitting, or in blowing their Noses.*

Science should address the issues of the common man, argued Franklin, and thus a study of flatulence is of greater practical importance than the loftiest philosophical texts. "Are there twenty Men in Europe at this Day, the happier, or even the easier, for any Knowledge they have pick'd out of Aristotle? What Comfort can the Vortices of Descartes give to a Man who has Whirlwinds in his Bowels!"

Franklin's "Letter to a Royal Academy"—known today by its nickname, "Fart Proudly"—is one of dozens of dirty essays by the Founding Father conspicuously absent from collections of his writings. Also missing: Ben's practical how-to guide, "Advice to a Friend on Choosing a Mistress."

YOU BETTER WATCH OUT
May 20, 325

On this day, in northwestern Anatolia, the Roman Emperor Constantine convened the First Council of Nicaea to discuss the nature of the Holy Trinity—specifically, whether the Church should consider Christ mortal or divine. Of the 300 or so attendees, only two disputed Christ's divinity. One was an Alexandrian priest named Arius. According to legend, as Arius argued his position before the council, a bishop in the back became enraged. Finally, he could no longer bear the blasphemies. He sat up, crossed the room, and punched Arius in the face.

That cantankerous bishop was Nicholas of Myra, later canonized as St. Nicholas—the man we know today as Santa Claus.

TODAY IN AVIATION HISTORY
May 21

On this day in 1927, Charles Lindbergh completed the first solo nonstop flight across the Atlantic Ocean.

Five years later, on May 21, 1932, Amelia Earhart completed the second solo nonstop flight across the Atlantic Ocean.

Exactly five years after that, Earhart departed on her first around-the-world flight. She was never heard from again.

IN PRODUCTION
May 22, 1951

In this inexorable era of superhero sequels, prequels, spinoffs, and crossovers, nothing quite excites DC fans—and then inevitably disappoints them—like hearing *Batman v. Commissioner* bandied about. This rumored next installment in the Batman franchise has been stirring up false hopes since May 22, 1951, when two Texas farmers, Ray and Edith Batman, filed an appeal against the Commissioner of Internal Revenue for a charge of tax evasion in the U.S. Court of Appeals. While the case rarely gets cited as a precedent in courtrooms nowadays, its comical title—suggesting a showdown between traditional allies Batman and Commissioner Gordon—still occasionally lights up corners of the Internet with production rumors.

DEFENESTRATION, PART I
May 23, 1618

To protest the removal of certain Protestant religious freedoms, an assembly of frustrated Protestants tossed three Catholic noblemen from the third-floor window of the Bohemian Chancellery, in an event known as the "Defenestration of Prague." (*Defenestrate:* to throw something out a window.) The fallout from this single rash act led to the Thirty Years' War, which resulted in eight million casualties.

All three dignitaries survived the fall by landing, allegedly, in a dung pile—though this latter detail was probably invented to humiliate them further. Also humiliating: the Holy Roman Emperor granted Philip Fabricius, the last to be flung, the new title Baron von Hohenfall—literally "Baron of Highfall."

DEFENESTRATION, PART II
May 24, 1920

On this day, President Paul Deschanel of France fell out of a window on the Orient Express dressed only in his pajamas.

The president, having grown overheated in his sleeper car during the night, struggled to crack a window for ventilation. Throwing all his weight into it, the stubborn pane suddenly gave out and dropped him onto the tracks near Lyons, as the train sped on without him. Barefoot and wearing only his green silk nightwear, Deschanel walked a mile in the darkness to the nearest signal box. "I am Monsieur Deschanel, president of the republic!" he shouted to the signalman. The signalman replied, "And I am the Emperor Napoleon."

THE STUPIDEST SONG EVER WRITTEN
May 25, 1980

When scoring the suicide scene of Captain Painless in the 1970 black comedy *M*A*S*H*, director Robert Altman had only one requirement: it had to be the "stupidest song ever written."

Altman took a crack at the lyrics himself but found he wasn't dumb enough to write them. His son had no such problem. "All is not lost," he told film composer Johnny Mandel. "I've got a 15-year-old kid who's a total idiot."

Altman's son Mike came up with the words in five minutes and Mandel set them to music. The result was "Suicide Is Painless," a florid three-minute track with such cringeworthy lines as "The sword of time will pierce our skins . . . / The pain grows stronger, watch it grin." Altman liked it so much he ran it over the opening credits as well.

When *M*A*S*H* got picked up as a TV series in 1972, "Suicide Is Painless" became its theme song. As the show surged in the Nielsen ratings, the track also climbed in the pop charts, finally peaking at #1 in the UK on May 25, 1980, above records by Paul McCartney, Peter Gabriel, and Elton John. Mike Altman, now 25, had become the most popular music-maker in the United Kingdom.

The toss-off track earned Mike far more than his father cleared for the film. While Robert made $70,000 for directing *M*A*S*H*, his son earned more than $1 million in royalties for writing the song.

RIGHT DAY
May 26, 1968

On this day, at precisely 6 a.m., Iceland switched from driving on the left-hand side of the road to the right, bringing it into line with most of Europe. At the appointed time, all Icelandic motorists came to a complete stop, carefully maneuvered over one lane, and began driving again. The only casualty from the changeover was a bicyclist's broken leg.

The day is remembered even now in Iceland as "Hægri dagurinn"—"Right Day."

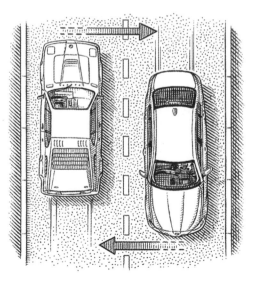

REQUIEM FOR A STARLING
May 27, 1784

On May 27, 1784, Wolfgang Amadeus Mozart made a new friend at a Viennese pet shop—a starling he taught to sing the opening theme of the third movement from his Piano Concerto no. 17 in G major. Despite sharping two Gs in the second measure, the bird apparently did a fine job. "Das war schön!"—"That was beautiful!"—Mozart exclaimed, and he bought the starling for 34 kreutzer.

The starling lived with Mozart for three years as his companion and muse. When it died in June 1787, the composer arranged an elaborate funeral and buried his departed friend in his backyard. He recited a poem over the grave:

> *A little fool lies here*
> *Whom I held dear—*
> *A starling in the prime*
> *Of his brief time*
> *Whose doom it was to drain*
> *Death's bitter pain . . .*
> *This no one can gainsay*
> *And I will lay*
> *That he is now on high,*
> *And from the sky,*
> *Praises me without pay*
> *In his friendly way.*
> *Yet unaware that death*
> *Has choked his breath,*
> *And thoughtless of the one*
> *Whose rime is thus well done.*

THE BIRTH OF SCIENCE
May 28, 585 BCE

Fighting between the perpetually warring Medes and Lydians stopped abruptly on May 28, 585 BCE, when the midday sun went black and the battlefield vanished for three minutes into unexpected darkness. The gods-fearing warriors laid down their arms and agreed to a truce.

Because astronomers can determine the dates of past solar eclipses, this battle is considered the oldest historical event whose date is known with absolute precision. It also may be the earliest predicted eclipse in human history: According to the Greek historian Herodotus, the celestial alignment was calculated in advance by the philosopher Thales of Miletus based on his study of heavenly movements. Isaac Asimov called Thales's calculation "the birth of science."

NO DANCING HERE
May 29, 1912

Bans on bodily gyrating go at least as far back as the ragtime era, when small American towns prohibited youngsters from boogying to the "Turkey Trot." (The Pope himself condemned the Trot for being sexually suggestive.) Even large cities like Philadelphia got in on the moral policing. On May 29, 1912, Edward Bok, the Pulitzer Prize–winning editor of the *Ladies' Home Journal,* fired fifteen employees from his Philly offices for dancing the Turkey Trot on their lunch break as a lesson to the others to spurn the Trot's temptation.

With every ban and denouncement, the Turkey Trot only increased in popularity among America's youth. "It is the prohibition," as Mark Twain once said, "that makes anything precious."

THE GLORY OF THE DIGESTING DUCK
May 30, 1739

Jacques de Vaucanson was an eighteenth-century French inventor who specialized in building *automata*—self-operating robots that mimicked natural movements to give the impression of being alive. On May 30, 1739, Vaucanson unveiled his masterpiece, the *Canard Digérateur,* or Digesting Duck—a life-sized, gold-plated robot that could eat, metabolize, and defecate kernels of grain. The French writer Voltaire later said, "Without . . . the duck of Vaucanson, you would have nothing to remind you of the glory of France."

POLE POSITION
May 31, 1949

Charley Lupica, a grocer from Cleveland, Ohio, began a four-month stay on a four-foot-wide platform atop a 60-foot flagpole, vowing to live there until baseball's Cleveland Indians won the championship pennant. Local Samaritans donated food, pajamas, a radio, and a television set. Mischief-makers pelted him with cans and firecrackers. He manned his perch through 100-degree days and cold, rainy nights, through his wedding anniversary and the birth of his fourth child. Even when his beloved Indians fell short of the pennant, Lupica was loath to leave his aerial vigil. At last, Bill Veeck, the Indians' owner, had the pole severed and towed with its inhabitant still aloft to Municipal Stadium for the final home game of the season. There, Lupica climbed down before 34,000 cheering fans and kissed home plate.

HOW MANY GODS DOES IT TAKE TO GUARD A DOORWAY?
June 1

The Romans had gods for a great many things, but not every god they had was great. For every Neptune (god of the sea) and Jupiter (god of the sky), they had a dozen Deveras (goddess of broomsticks) and Cloacinas (goddess of the Roman sewer system). Worshippers of the so-called "minor gods" of Roman mythology mark June 1 a red-letter day: it is dedicated to Cardea, the goddess of door hinges.

Rounding out the Holy Trinity of Roman doorways are Limentinus (god of thresholds) and Forculus (god of doors). St. Augustine mocked the Romans' excessive door security: he noted that while pagans need three gods to guard an entrance, Christians require only one.

SYMPATHY FOR THE CHOIRBOY
June 2, 1953

Rolling Stones' wild man Keith Richards—a tough-as-nails rocker once described as "a capering streak of living gristle who ought to be exhibited as a warning to the young of what drugs can do to you"—began his career as an angelic high soprano in an all-boys choir. "Keef" distinguished himself at Wentworth Primary School, and on June 2, 1953, at age nine, sang in a choir at Queen Elizabeth II's coronation. When his voice broke a few years later—embarrassingly, during a live performance—the chorister was canned, and he began a rebellious streak that lasted long, *long* into old age. Richards said that the day he was thrown out of choir was the day he "stopped being a good boy."

SODA POP
June 3, 1970

The Kinks released two versions of their 1970 hit "Lola": the "Coca-Cola" version and the "cherry cola" version. Because of a strict BBC ban on product advertising, the original lyric—"I met her in a club down in old Soho / Where you drink champagne and it tastes just like Coca-Cola"—had to be altered for radio play. On June 3, 1970, a week before the song's release, Kinks front man Ray Davies interrupted the band's American tour to fly 7,000 miles round-trip between New York and London, in a single day, to overdub two words—"cherry cola"—in place of the trademarked pop. Ultimately, the Coca-Cola "Lola" appeared on the album, while the generic cherry cola version was pressed into the 7-inch single used for radio play.

DEAD AT THE REINS
June 4, 1923

Frank Hayes entered the 1923 Belmont steeplechase a 20–1 outsider. He was a horse trainer by trade, not a jockey, and such was his shock when he pulled ahead in the fourth lap that he had a heart attack and promptly died. His limp body remained in its saddle for three more laps, and Hayes rode on to victory atop the still-galloping mare. It was the first—and last—win of his career.

A PAIR FOR THE AGES
June 5, 2012

In a spirited act of shared humdrummery, the city of Boring, Oregon (population: 8,000), accepted a proposal from Dull, Scotland (population: 80), to pair up as official sister cities.

"Be it known throughout the world that Boring, Oregon, U.S.A., and Dull, Perthshire, Scotland, U.K., are hereby recognized as paired communities," read a declaration to the Boring congregation. "Boring, Oregon, and Dull, Scotland—A Pair for the Ages!"

Not to be left out, the Australian shire of Bland got in on the action two years later. Together with Boring and Dull they formed the "League of Extraordinary Communities" in 2014.

JUDGE CRATER, CALL YOUR OFFICE
June 6, 1939

On this day, Judge Crater—"The Missingest Man in New York"—was declared legally dead, nine years after last being seen leaving a Manhattan chophouse on West 45th Street. His life as a punch line, however, was just beginning.

For decades, comedians and class clowns could get a reliable laugh with a well-timed joke about Joseph Crater, the mob-tied State Supreme Court justice who mysteriously vanished in 1930. "*Finally,* Judge Crater returns," a radio comedy character might jibe his tardy friend. "Judge Crater, please call your office," a miscreant might say into the school intercom before being chased down by the superintendent. The joke, of course, was that Judge Crater would never be calling his office. Judge Crater would never be calling anyone.

Crater's disappearance remained a mystery until 2005, when police uncovered a handwritten letter in an envelope marked "Do not open until my death," left behind by a 91-year-old grandmother from Queens. She claimed her husband learned over drinks with a cop and a cabbie that the two had killed the judge in 1930 and buried him under the Coney Island boardwalk, at the current site of the New York Aquarium. The last Judge Crater joke writes itself: he sleeps with the fishes.

TO WINSTON, FROM WINSTON
June 7, 1899

For a time in the early twentieth century, the only Winston Churchill worth noting was an American romance novelist from St. Louis. In 1898, this Midwestern Churchill began a two-decade run as America's top-selling author, producing 11 novels, 4 stage plays, and 1 memoir—all bestsellers—and amassing one of the largest literary fortunes of his day.

It was during this extraordinary run that another Winston Churchill, a 25-year-old officer with the British Army (and Britain's future Prime Minister), began coming to prominence as an author in his own right. On June 7, 1899, the British Churchill wrote to his American namesake proposing a way to avoid confusion as they embarked on independent literary careers under the same moniker:

> *Mr. Winston Churchill presents his compliments to Mr. Winston Churchill, and begs to draw his attention to a matter which concerns them both. He has learnt from the Press notices that Mr. Winston Churchill proposes to bring out another novel, entitled Richard Carvel, which is certain to have a considerable sale both in England and America. Mr. Winston Churchill is also the author of a novel now being published in serial form in Macmillan's Magazine, and for which he anticipates some sale both in England and America . . .*
>
> *He has no doubt that Mr. Winston Churchill will recognise from this letter—if indeed by no other means—that there is grave danger of his works being mistaken for those of Mr. Winston Churchill. . . .*

In future to avoid mistakes as far as possible, Mr. Winston Churchill has decided to sign all published articles, stories, or other works, "Winston Spencer Churchill," and not "Winston Churchill" as formerly. He trusts that this arrangement will commend itself to Mr. Winston Churchill, and he ventures to suggest, with a view to preventing further confusion which may arise out of this extraordinary coincidence, that both Mr. Winston Churchill and Mr. Winston Churchill should insert a short note in their respective publications explaining to the public which are the works of Mr. Winston Churchill and which those of Mr. Winston Churchill.

The other Churchill replied:

Mr. Winston Churchill appreciates the courtesy of Mr. Winston Churchill in adopting the name of "Winston Spencer Churchill" in his books, articles, etc. Mr. Winston Churchill makes haste to add that, had he possessed any other names, he would certainly have adopted one of them.

ARE WE BORING YOU, MR. RODALE?
June 8, 1971

When Jerome "Mr. Organic" Rodale appeared on *The Dick Cavett Show,* he boasted that he had decided to live to one hundred years old. "I never felt better in my life!" he proclaimed. He didn't even make it to the next commercial break.

The seventy-two-year-old health guru suffered a heart attack on camera a few minutes later. As Cavett switched the conversation to his other guest, the New York columnist Pete Hamill, Rodale's head suddenly bobbed to one side. "Are we boring you, Mr. Rodale?" Cavett jibed. "This looks bad," whispered Hamill. Next thing, Cavett was at the edge of the stage, yelling out that tired old vaudeville line, "Is there a doctor in the audience?" But this was no joke.

Two medical interns rushed to the stage and administered CPR, but their attempts to revive Rodale fell short. The once-robust health expert was already dead.

ABC's pre-taped episode was never broadcast, and the footage has been lost, but it has since become the subject of a phenomenon known as the "Mandela Effect." It seems Cavett's description of Rodale's death the next day planted a false memory of the event in his collective viewership. To this day, many still insist they remember seeing Mr. Organic die on television, although it's positively impossible. (The phenomenon is named after Nelson Mandela: Many people apparently "remember" Mandela dying in prison in the 1980s, though he actually died in 2013, 23 years after being freed.)

DRAMATIC IRONY
June 9, 1893

American actor Edwin Booth, the premier Shakespearean of his day, was connected to two major tragedies involving the same Washington theater. In April 1865, his younger brother John Wilkes, another successful stage actor of the Booth theatrical family, killed President Abraham Lincoln at Ford's Theatre with a bullet to the back of the head. Three decades later, on June 9, 1893—the day of Edwin Booth's funeral—a support beam in the basement of Ford's Theatre buckled, and the entire building collapsed, killing 22 people.

POLLY WANT A #$@&%*!
June 10, 1845

U.S. President Andrew Jackson's pet parrot, Poll, squawked like a sailor. At his owner's funeral, the red-tailed African Grey let loose such a tirade of profanity that the organizers had to remove him from the ceremony. The Reverend William Menefee Norment, who presided over the service, said Poll's "perfect gusts of cuss words" left the funeral attendees "horrified and awed at the bird's lack of reverence."

Those who knew Jackson had a good idea where Poll picked up the habit.

HIS SATANIC MAJESTY
June 11, 1968

During a wee hour session for "Sympathy for the Devil," a fire broke out in the Rolling Stones' recording studio. "I was playing organ, looked up, and there was this ring of fire on the ceiling," said session keyboardist Nicky Hopkins.

While many pointed to Lucifer as the likely culprit, the blaze was actually caused by Jean-Luc Godard, the French filmmaker, who was documenting the sessions. He had taped flammable tissue paper over the ceiling lights for mood effect.

ELLIS, D.
June 12, 1970

Dock Ellis spent the morning of June 12, 1970, doing what he always did on his day off: the Pittsburgh Pirates pitcher took a hit of LSD and settled in for a long, strange trip in the privacy of his Los Angeles home.

He woke an hour later to his girlfriend waving the sports page in front of his face, pointing to the Pirates' game schedule. Ellis had mixed up his dates: not only were the Pirates scheduled to play in San Diego that afternoon, but Ellis was slated to pitch. In a delirium of hallucination, the ballplayer rushed to Los Angeles International Airport to catch a 3:30 flight. He arrived in San Diego at 4:30, ninety minutes before game time.

As Ellis took the mound, the world melted and warped before him:

> *The ball was small sometimes, the ball was large sometimes, sometimes I saw the catcher, sometimes I didn't. . . . I started having a crazy idea in the fourth inning that Richard Nixon was the home plate umpire, and once I thought I was pitching a baseball to Jimi Hendrix, who to me was holding a guitar and swinging it over the plate.*

Despite his erratic performance (he walked eight batters and plunked one in the back), Ellis managed to get through all nine innings and win the game 2–0. Incredibly, he had also kept the Padres hitless. The 25-year-old right-hander, high as a kite, had accomplished one of the rarest feats in baseball: he had pitched a no-hitter.

THE AMEN BREAK
June 13, 1969

The most sampled musical track of all time is a mediocre record called "Amen, Brother," recorded on June 13, 1969, by a middling funk group called The Winstons.

In the 1980s, as hip hop began heating up in New York, a local disc jockey, looking for a way to transition seamlessly between songs during sets, stumbled across the Winstons' track. At the song's 1:26 mark, drummer G. C. Coleman performs a six-second drum solo. The DJ edited this into a space-filler and shared it with others in the burgeoning movement. Before long, the four-bar snare-and-cymbal sequence—the so-called "Amen break"—became a go-to drum sample in the early hip-hop scene.

Since 1985, Coleman's solo has been looped into some 2,000 songs—in hip hop and beyond—including N.W.A's "Straight Outta Compton," Lupe Fiasco's "Streets on Fire," Slipknot's "Eyeless," and the Pixies' "La La Love You." The rhythm is so ubiquitous, in fact, that if you were to drop a beat right now (go ahead), you'd likely be riffing on Coleman.

Despite the song's success, The Winstons never received any royalties. G. C. Coleman, the most sampled musician in the world, died broke and homeless in Atlanta in 2006.

HAREBRAINED
June 14, 1952

Paul-Félix Armand-Delille, a distinguished bacteriologist known for his work on malaria during World War I, was 77 years old and long retired when he read in the papers that Australia was using virus inoculation to curb its wild rabbit population.

Armand-Delille had a little rabbit problem of his own—his 700-acre private estate in the north of France was overrun with them—so on June 14, 1952, the scientist inoculated two of the pests with the *Myxomatosis cuniculi* virus in the hope that it would rid his property of the agricultural nuisance once and for all.

Within two months, the virus killed 98 percent of the rabbits on his estate. Within a year, it wiped out 45 percent of the rabbits in France. The virus spread into Luxembourg, Belgium, the Netherlands, Italy, Germany, and Spain, and by the end of 1954 had become responsible for hundreds of millions of rabbit deaths across the continent. Armand-Delille had single-handedly brought about the collapse of Western Europe's rabbit population.

Armand-Delille was denounced by hunting and breeding interests, who saw their industry crumble. He was exalted at the same time by farmers and foresters, who saw their industry boom. One side sued him for 5,000 francs. The other awarded him a gold medal.

A FUGITIVE ACT
June 15, 1824

On June 15, 1824, at the age of 15, future U.S. President Andrew Johnson and his brother ran away from their tailor indenture-ship, to which they were bound for about 10 years. The following advertisement ran in the North Carolina *Gazette*:

> *Ten Dollars Reward. Ran away from the subscriber, two apprentice boys, legally bound, named William and Andrew Johnson . . . [payment] to any person who will deliver said apprentices to me in Raleigh, or I will give the above reward for Andrew Johnson alone.*

The fugitives were never caught. Later on in his political career, Johnson became a supporter of the Fugitive Slave Act, which required states to turn in runaways.

PECKING ORDER
June 16, 1903

The term "pecking order" refers to behavior exhibited in chicken coops: to assert dominance, the birds peck at each other's eyes. Tennessee inventor Andrew Jackson, Jr. aimed to subvert battles for coop supremacy. On this day, Jackson patented chicken eye-glasses, a contraption featuring two composite glass lenses fitted inside a wire frame. The spectacles rested on the bridge of the beak and helped thwart peevish peckers.

The rounded frames and thick, nerdy rims didn't actually forestall chicken fighting, but they did confer an air of snobbish academia to the scuffle. If nothing else, watching chicken fights became a lot more enjoyable.

FOUL MISCONDUCT
June 17, 2016

On this day, Swedish soccer player Adam Lindin Ljungkvist received a red card and an ejection for breaking wind on the pitch.

"I had a bad stomach, so I simply let go," said Ljungkvist, whose flatulence came across as "deliberate provocation" to the referee. "Then I received two yellow cards and then red. . . . It's the strangest thing I have ever experienced in football."

The whistle-happy ref had seen stranger: "Once there was a player who stood and peed next to the pitch. I showed him a yellow card, too."

"HIKING THE APPALACHIAN TRAIL"
June 18, 2009

On this day, South Carolina Governor Mark Sanford went missing. For four days, nobody knew where he was—not his staff, not his security detail, not even his own wife and children. Finally, on June 22, Sanford's spokesman announced the governor had resurfaced: he was reportedly hiking the Appalachian Trail, a public trekking route in the Eastern United States, and was off the grid for several days.

But Sanford wasn't on a woodsy jaunt at all. He was in Buenos Aires visiting his Argentinian lover. A reporter, tipped off by an anonymous source, confronted Sanford at the airport upon his return and cornered him in an off-guard interview. That afternoon, in the rotunda of the South Carolina Statehouse, Sanford confessed his whole unsavory encounter and resigned from his position as chairman of the Republican Governors Association.

Though devastating to Sanford's presidential prospects, the episode at least brought a colorful new colloquialism to the English language. To "hike the Appalachian Trail" is now slang for engaging in an extramarital affair.

A BIRTHDAY GIFT
June 19, 1891

Annie Ide had the tragic misfortune of being born on Christmas Day. The 12-year-old daughter of Henry Clay Ide, the U.S. Commissioner to Samoa, hated sharing her birthday with her family's Christmas festivities, and longed to have a day all to herself. Her wish came true on June 19, 1891, when *Treasure Island* author Robert Louis Stevenson, a friend of her father's, deeded his own birthday of November 13 to young Annie. He typed up the following legal document, formally transferring his birthday rights to the unhappy girl:

I, Robert Louis Stevenson . . . In consideration that Miss A. H. Ide, daughter of H. C. Ide, in the town of St Johnsbury, in the County of Caledonia, in the State of Vermont, United States of America, was born, out of all reason, upon Christmas Day, and is therefore, out of all justice, denied the consolation and profit of a Proper Birthday;

And considering that I, the said Robert Louis Stevenson, have attained an age when O, we never mention it, and that I have now no further use for a birthday of any description . . .

Have transferred, and do hereby transfer to the said A. H. Ide, All and Whole of my rights and privileges in the 13th day of November, formerly my birthday, now, hereby, and henceforth, the birthday of the said A. H. Ide, to have, hold, exercise and enjoy the same in the customary manner, by the sporting of fine raiment, eating of rich meats and receipt of gifts . . .

Robert Louis Stevenson

LADY SMOKERS
June 20, 1921

On this day, Paul B. Johnson, a representative from Mississippi, introduced a bill banning women from smoking in public. The crude habit degraded ladies, Johnson said, even "worse than whisky," and he objected to seeing the fairer sex indulge in such low class behavior. "I saw a young lady on F Street take a cigarette out of the hand of the young man she was walking with and take a puff herself. It was the last straw."

The bill, which proposed to fine lady smokers $25 for the first offense, plus $100 per cigarette for every subsequent offense, gained support in the all-male House of Representatives. However, it was ultimately a group of women—mothers, grandmothers, secretaries, and flappers, newly enfranchised with the right to vote (the Nineteenth Amendment passed the previous year)—that blocked the bill in a public hearing in July with a vote of 24 to 1.

WHAT DO YOU THINK OF MY BLOOMERS?
June 21, 1895

The June 21, 1895, edition of the *Newark Sunday Advocate* reported a recent breach of dress code at a women's cycling club in Chicago. To the end of the article, the author appended a list of etiquette "Don'ts" for female bicycle riders. A few highlights:

Don't wear loud-hued leggings.
Don't cultivate a "bicycle face."
Don't imagine everybody is looking at you.
Don't ask, "What do you think of my bloomers?"
Don't discuss bloomers with every man you know.
Don't scream if you meet a cow. If she sees you first, she will run.

PORTMANTEAU LAND
June 22, 1913

In an article titled "New Arrivals in Portmanteau Land," *The New York Times* described recent additions to the lexicon of hybrid words:

Alcoholiday (leisure time spent while drinking)
Brunch (a meal that is too late to call breakfast and too early to call lunch)
Bungaloafer (a gentleman who takes his ease in his bungalow)
Cathletic (a man of the cloth who is also obsessed with outdoor sports)

UMPIRE ABUSE
June 23, 1917

Babe Ruth was ejected from a baseball game on June 23, 1917, for punching the home plate umpire, Clarence "Brick" Owens, in the head over a disputed call. "Brick" was a serial abuse victim: Over the years he'd taken bats to the head and cabbages to the face, was once followed to his hotel and attacked by a batter he called out on strikes, and often left games by police escort. He picked up his nickname when a fan hurled a brick at him from the stands.

THE DANCING PLAGUE
June 24, 1374

On this day, thousands of people in the town of Aachen, Germany, suddenly began dancing uncontrollably, in the first major outbreak of what scholars call the "dancing plague." The mass hysteria spread across central Europe, causing men, women, and children to dance for days in wild delirium until collapsing from exhaustion.

A 1625 poem from the Straussburgh Chronicle of Kleinkawel describes a later outbreak of the epidemic:

Amidst our people here is come
The madness of the dance.
In every town there now are some
Who fall upon a trance.
It drives them ever night and day,
They scarcely stop for breath,
Till some have dropped along the way
And some are met by death.

At the time, the dancing plague was thought to be a curse sent by St. Vitus, the patron saint of dancers and epileptics. No scientific cause has ever been confirmed for the phenomenon.

A FATAL LOVE TRIANGLE
June 25, 1906

Stanford White was one of New York's most celebrated Gilded Age architects, the man behind Washington Square's triumphal arch, the Tiffany & Co. building, and the stretch of Beaux Arts mansions along Fifth Avenue. His masterpiece was Madison Square Garden (since demolished and rebuilt elsewhere under the same name), an 8,000-capacity arena that hosted boxing matches, political conventions, and the Barnum and Ringling circuses. It would also be the scene of White's murder.

A notorious philanderer, White carried on affairs with the wives of New York's richest men—and the richer he got, the more reckless he became. In 1905 he became embroiled in a love triangle with Evelyn Nesbit, a popular chorus girl, and her millionaire husband Harry Kendall Thaw. On June 25, 1906, Thaw tracked down White on the rooftop of his own Madison Square Garden and aimed a pistol at his face. "You've ruined my wife," he said. He then fired three shots.

THE ADVOCATE
June 26, 1659

Europe has a long history of putting animals on trial. On June 26, 1659, an Italian farmer named J. B. Pestalozzi brought charges against some local caterpillars for trespassing on his fields and damaging them. The accused were assigned an attorney, Cesare de Peverello, who argued that his clients have the right to pursue happiness where they will. The court agreed, so long as the exercise of that right "does not destroy or impair the happiness of man, to whom all lower animals are subject." The caterpillars were told to keep off Pestalozzi's fields.

TAKE ME OUT TO THE BALLGAME
June 27, 1940

Jack Norworth, author of the baseball anthem "Take Me Out to the Ballgame," was never much of a fan. He attended his first ballgame on June 27, 1940—32 years after writing the song—and only because he felt obliged: it was "Jack Norworth Day" at the stadium.

A WRONG TURN AND A CHEESE PASTRY
June 28, 1914

After squandering an opportunity to assassinate the Archduke Franz Ferdinand in Sarajevo on the morning of June 28, 1914—a combination of nerves, bad timing, and a malfunctioning grenade—Gavrilo Princip gave up and followed a different pleasure: he went to Moritz Schiller's delicatessen on Franz Joseph Street to grab some lunch.

Just as Princip bit into his *burek,* a savory Bosnian cheese pastry, the Archduke's vehicle pulled up in front of the deli. Ferdinand's chauffeur had become lost in the Sarajevo backstreets and taken a wrong turn onto Franz Joseph, the busy thoroughfare he meant to avoid, and in trying to reverse had stalled the engine. The assassin couldn't believe his luck. He walked out and fired easily into the open car, hitting the Archduke in the jugular.

Ferdinand's assassination triggered a series of events that led directly to World War I, which killed 37 million people, destroyed most of the world's imperial dynasties, destituted Germany, and left a chip on the shoulder of a young German corporal named Adolf Hitler, who vowed lifelong revenge on his foes. If it weren't for a disoriented chauffeur—and a sudden craving for a cheese pastry—oh, how different our world would look today.

DON WE NOW OUR GAY ERRATUM
June 29, 2008

On this day, *OneNewsNow,* the media arm of the ultraconservative American Family Association, ran a headline with the gaffe, "Homosexual Eases into 100 Final at Olympic Trials," thanks to an algorithm programmed to change all instances of the word *gay* to *homosexual.*

The article on Olympic sprinter Tyson Gay went on to say that "Tyson Homosexual easily won his semifinal for the 100 meters at the U.S. Olympic track and field trials," even though a day earlier "Homosexual misjudged the finish in his opening heat and had to scramble to finish fourth."

THE LIVING DEAD
June 30, 2010

In 1977, a 22-year-old Indian man named Lal Bihari was denied a bank loan. The reason: according to government records, Bihari was dead. With a little digging, Bihari discovered that his uncle had forged his death certificate and bribed a government official in order to seize Bihari's land. Surprisingly, this is a common practice among antagonized family members in India—especially in the overcrowded region of Uttar Pradesh, where land is particularly scarce. Bihari became a spokesman for these erroneously departed and formed the Uttar Pradesh Association of Dead People, an organization that helps "dead" citizens on a track back to legal existence.

On June 30, 2010, hundreds of UPADP members marched in a "Day of Rebirth" rally to prove to the world that they are, in fact, alive, despite what the records say. The rally helped Bihari reclaim his living status and fetch others from clerical oblivion. One resurrected Uttar Pradeshi said, "My own son had killed me off. If it had not been for Lal Bihari, I would still be dead."

THE FIRST CAT VIDEO
July 1, 1894

When anthropologists of the future study our browser histories (they will—don't think they won't), they'll deduce a feline worship on par with the Ancient Egyptians. We have one man to thank for that. On this day, Thomas Edison produced "The Boxing Cats," the world's first-ever cat video. Filmed at his studio in West Orange, New Jersey, the 21-second clip shows two gloved kitties trading hooks and jabs inside a litter box–sized ring, as a grinning human referee looks on. Edison's caption reads, "A glove contest between trained cats. A very comical and amusing subject, and is sure to create a great laugh." The man was *seriously* ahead of his time.

THE GREAT ANNIVERSARY FESTIVAL
July 2, 1776

On this date, America declared its independence—not, as the history books would have it, on the Fourth of July. (That was the day the Declaration was *ratified*.) In a letter to his wife, John Adams naively predicted, "The Second of July, 1776, will be the most memorable Epocha, in the History of America. I am apt to believe that it will be celebrated, by succeeding Generations, as the great anniversary Festival."

THE LAST GREAT AUK
July 3, 1844

Like its cousin the penguin, the great auk was a powerful swimmer but hopelessly clumsy on land, which made it an easy and irresistible target for poachers. Over three centuries, the three-foot-tall flightless bird was hunted to extinction for its nourishing meat (to fatten up sailors on long journeys) and its feathery down (to fatten up pillows and mattresses in Europe). On July 3, 1844, European fishermen cornered the world's last pair of great auks on a small island off the coast of Iceland and slaughtered them. During the chase, one of the hunters accidentally crushed the last auk egg with his boot—literally stamping out the species forever.

DEAD PRESIDENTS
July 4

For all its patriotic symbolism, the Fourth of July is actually an unlucky date for U.S. presidents. Thomas Jefferson and John Adams died within hours of each other on July 4, 1826, exactly 50 years after the adoption of the Declaration of Independence; James Monroe, the fifth president, shuffled off five years later on July 4, 1831; and Zachary Taylor, who died on July 9, 1850, took ill at an Independence Day dinner on the fourth—allegedly from arsenic poisoning.

FRESH PEPPER?
July 5, 1819

Counterfeit black pepper was a real problem in nineteenth-century Britain. To get the best bang for their buck, pepper purveyors often cut their product with "pepper dust" swept up from their warehouse floors. This potpourri could include everything from fine pepper powder to dirt, soot, dust—one particle indistinguishable from the other in the ragbag mix. Britain finally cracked down on pesky pepper counterfeiters with the Pepper Act of 1819:

> *"Be it therefore enacted, that from and after the said 5th day of July, 1819, if any commodity or commodities, substance or substances, shall be prepared or manufactured by any person or persons in imitation of pepper, shall be mixed with pepper, or sold or delivered as and for or as a substitute for pepper . . . together with all pepper with which the same shall be mixed shall be forfeited, together with the package or packages containing the same, and shall and may be seized by any officer or officers of excise; and the persons preparing, manufacturing, mixing as aforesaid, selling, exposing to sale, or delivering the same, or having the same in his, her, or their custody or possession as aforesaid, shall forfeit and lose the sum of one hundred pounds."*

TIME OUT OF MIND
July 6, 1189

The phrase *time immemorial* refers to a vague period beyond the reach of memory—indefinitely old, way back in the hazy mists of time. In English law, however, the phrase has a more definite meaning: *Time immemorial* literally means anything that happened before July 6, 1189. That was the date of King Richard I's coronation; His Majesty's reign is considered the limit of legal memory.

SURE SHOT
July 7, 1912

At the 1912 Stockholm Olympics, 26-year-old George S. Patton—the man who would one day command U.S. military operations in Europe during World War II—placed fifth in the men's pentathlon. His worst event, ironically, was shooting.

He blamed his poor performance on his gun: Patton claimed that because he used a larger caliber than his opponents, his shots had passed right through the holes he'd already blasted in previous rounds. That's why only 17 of his 20 bullets seemed to have hit the target.

SUNDAE BEST
July 8, 1881

On July 8, 1881, George Hallauer walked into a Wisconsin soda fountain and asked the clerk, Edward C. Berner, to top off his bowl of ice cream with flavored syrup, an ingredient usually reserved for carbonated sodas. Berner obliged and soon began offering the concoction to other customers—but only on Sundays.

Like alcohol, soda was considered immoral and could not be sold on the Lord's Day. Unlike saloons, however, soda fountains were still allowed to remain open, so long as they didn't push their "intoxicating" soft drink when church let out. Many shops closed Sunday anyway for lack of business, but now, with the new soda-less treat—later termed the "ice cream sundae"—Sundays at the soda fountain were suddenly hopping.

PAPER REVOLUTION
July 9, 1887

Fortunately for ice cream eaters, the invention of the paper napkin followed close behind the creation of the sundae. At the annual dinner for the John Dickinson Stationery company on July 9, 1887, guests found flimsy, low-grade paper sheets to the left of their forks instead of the standard cloth towels—history's first recorded use of paper napkins. This rectangular repository for spontaneous ideas and dabs of tomato sauce was part of a revolution in the paper industry that also saw the invention of toilet paper rolls (1879), paper plates (1904), and paper cups (1907)—all the fixings for during *and* after meals.

WHAT'S IN A NAME?
July 10, 1882

Texas governor Big Jim Hogg gave his sons typical down-home American names—Will, Mike, and Tom—but with his daughter he got more creative. She told the story of that fateful night of her birth, July 10, 1882:

> *My grandfather Stinson lived fifteen miles from Mineola. . . . When he learned of his granddaughter's name he came trotting to town as fast as he could to protest but it was too late. The christening had taken place, and Ima I was to remain.*

Throughout her life, Ima Hogg asked to be addressed as Miss Hogg, and when signing her name she would make sure to scribble the first word illegibly.

The legend that she had a sister named Ura is false.

WOMEN IN THE WORKPLACE
July 11, 1971

On this day, the U.S. Department of Agriculture announced a study to determine whether a woman's place is, in fact, in the home. With a $19,520 grant from the Agricultural Research Service, Cornell researchers proposed to analyze the cost benefits of housewifery versus workforce employment for married women, in an effort to make scientific sense of the growing feminist movement. The results were deemed inconclusive.

CALIFORNIA: A LAND WITHOUT MEN
July 12, 1510

Garci Rodríguez de Montalvo coined the word "California" in his fantasy novel *The Adventures of Esplandián*. In the book, published July 12, 1510, California is an island inhabited only by women warriors and guarded by a flock of wild griffins trained to kill any man they find.

> *They fed [the griffins] with the men whom they took prisoners, and with the boys to whom they gave birth. . . . Every man who landed on the island was immediately devoured by these griffins; and although they had had enough, none the less would they seize them, and carry them high up in the air in their flight; and when they were tired of carrying them, would let them fall anywhere.*

Hernán Cortés was charmed by Montalvo's depiction of the mythical island, and in 1534 the Spanish Conquistador sent out two ships in search of it. His men anchored off the western coast of Mexico, in what is today Baja California. They went ashore for water but were never heard from again.

BEST IN SHOW
July 13, 1871

The world of show cats and cat shows began with Harrison Weir, author of the classic feline primping manual *Our Cats and All About Them,* and the man regarded today as "The Father of the Cat Fancy." Weir organized the world's first cat show on July 13, 1871, at London's Crystal Palace, awarding medals in 54 categories to 170 specimens of Manx, French-African, French and Persian longhair, English shorthair, and other rare breeds. The show's main attraction—which earned no medals but plenty of gasps—was a pair of Siamese cats, a breed never before been seen in England. One attendee called it "a nightmare kind of a cat."

Not all the contestants belonged to elegant pedigrees. According to an account by *Pearson's Magazine,* Weir had a hard time convincing England's cat fanciers to part with their pets for the day. "Then someone discovered that the Palace cellars were full of cats and kittens and mice, so a few workmen were set to work cat-hunting there." Thus, to round out his exhibition of fancy felines, Weir slipped in a handful of homely strays.

BETTER LATE THAN NEVER
July 14, 1912

Shizo Kanakuri, the former world record–holding marathoner, went missing on this day during the 1912 Stockholm Olympic marathon only to turn up again 54 years later and finish the race.

Kanakuri arrived in Stockholm in 1912 after a rough 18-day trip from Japan, traveling first by ship to North Korea, then by Trans-Siberian Railway to Moscow, then by successive trains, ships, and carriages to Sweden. By the time he disembarked he was malnourished and out of shape. (The only exercise he got on his journey was jogging around the train stations he stopped at.) Worse still, the day of the marathon, July 14, 1912, was an unexpected scorcher. Weak and dehydrated, Kanakuri struggled through the first half of the race. At around the 16-mile mark, he lost consciousness. A local Swedish family took him in and nursed him back to health, after which the marathoner silently returned to Japan, ashamed of his failure. Because he neglected to check back in with the Olympic Committee, Swedish authorities considered him a missing person.

It took 54 years before a Swedish racing official spotted Kanakuri's name in newsprint; Kanakuri had not only been alive all this time, it seemed, but had also raced in two subsequent Olympic marathons. The Swedish National Olympic Committee invited him back to complete his race, which, in March 1967, he did. His official time: 54 years, 8 months, 6 days, 5 hours, 32 minutes, and 20.379 seconds.

"It was a long trip," Kanakuri said. "Along the way, I got married, had six children, and ten grandchildren."

AND THE HIPPOS WERE BOILED IN THEIR TANKS
July 15, 1984

At Karlsruhe Zoo in West Germany, a 30-year-old female elephant named Rani reached her trunk through her cage and turned on a hot water tap in the hippopotamus tank next door. Three hippos were boiled alive.

The incident occurred nearly 40 years to the day after another case of negligent hippocide. On July 6, 1944, a fire broke out at the Hartford Circus, killing dozens of circus animals, including several hippos. Their deaths inspired the title of Jack Kerouac's and William S. Burroughs's collaborative novel, *And the Hippos Were Boiled in Their Tanks*.

KISS OF DEATH
July 16, 1439

To curtail the spread of plague, King Henry VI banned all kissing in England—even the ritual smooches of His Highness's hand.

Either the British citizenry didn't heed the ban or Shakespeare didn't do his research: In his three-part play *Henry VI* (1591), set during the monarch's reign, characters kiss each other some 16 times. (No wonder half of Europe got wiped out.)

THE DOCTOR AND THE DETECTOR
July 17, 1881

The first physician summoned after U.S. President James Garfield's assassination attempt was Dr. D. Willard Bliss—a man who the District of Columbia Medical Society had expelled as a quack. (The "D" stood for Doctor—his actual name.) For weeks, Bliss poked and prodded the president's gaping abdomen with his unclean hands (he was notorious in the medical field for denying the science of antiseptics), searching for the potentially fatal bullet. After his groping yielded nothing, Bliss summoned Alexander Graham Bell, the inventor of the telephone. Rumor had it that Bell had a new gizmo that could detect metal.

Bell arrived in Washington and began testing his invention. "We get better and better results," Bell wrote his wife on July 17, 1881. "Yesterday we were able to locate a bullet held in the clenched hand—and last night I located successfully a bullet hidden in a bag filled with cotton-waste. This looks promising." But when Bell applied his metal detector to Garfield's body it went haywire; the machine seemed to think Garfield was one big lump of metal. Bliss called Bell's invention a failure, sent him packing, and kept on with his unsanitized prodding. He never found the bullet, and Garfield died of his injuries two months later.

Bell tinkered and fiddled with his metal detector for months trying to figure out the cause of the malfunction. It turns out it was in perfect working order the whole time; it had been detecting the metal spring mattress upon which the president lay.

UNDELIVERED EULOGY
July 18, 1969

On this date, two days before the *Apollo 11* moon landing, White House speechwriter William Safire prepared a contingency speech to be read by President Richard Nixon in the event of a lunar marooning:

> *Fate has ordained that the men who went to the moon to explore in peace will stay on the moon to rest in peace. These brave men, Neil Armstrong and Edwin Aldrin, know that there is no hope for their recovery. . . . They will be mourned by their families and friends; they will be mourned by the nation; they will be mourned by the people of the world; they will be mourned by a Mother Earth that dared send two of her sons into the unknown. . . .*

Fortunately Nixon never had to read it.

JANE THE QUEEN
July 19, 1553

On this day, Lady Jane Grey was ousted from the British throne by her covetous cousin Mary I—a.k.a. "Bloody Mary"—after only nine days of reign.

Sixteen-year-old Jane never wanted to be queen and was more than happy to return to her former life. But her cousin wouldn't allow that. Because Jane had already signed some documents "Jane the Queen," she was accused of treason and beheaded.

DARK'S PROPHECY
July 20, 1969

Baseball hall-of-famer Gaylord Perry was a gangly 6-foot-4 pitcher better known for his spitball than his swing. Perry's hitting was so awful, in fact (lifetime batting average: .131), that it inspired a bit of baseball lore. In the spring of 1962, Perry was taking batting practice when newspaperman Harry Jupiter made an admiring comment to Perry's manager, Alvin Dark, about Perry's improved swing. Dark scoffed, "Man will land on the moon before Gaylord Perry hits a home run."

Five years later, on July 20, 1969, Perry was standing on the mound in the top of the third inning when Candlestick Park erupted: Neil Armstrong had just stepped on the moon. In the bottom of the inning, with two outs and nobody on base, Perry came up to the plate and blasted the first home run of his career. "Alvin was right," Perry later said, "but only by an hour."

THE HEROSTRATUS EFFECT
July 21, 356 BC

On this date, a young Greek named Herostratus burned down the Temple of Artemis, one of the Seven Wonders of the Ancient World, in a vainglorious attempt to immortalize his name. To deter similar-minded fame hounds, Greek authorities condemned Herostratus to *damnatio memoriae*—"condemnation of memory"—a Greek law banning the mention of a criminal's name, thereby ensuring them a legacy of obscurity. It backfired. The mere act of declaring Herostratus's name unspeakable only gave it more recognition, and as it passed through the years, it came to describe all notoriety-seekers. Today, the word "herostratic" refers to a person who commits a crime just to become famous.

Though her temple lay destroyed, Artemis was unscathed. The Greek goddess of childbirth was said to be 300 miles away overseeing the delivery of Alexander the Great, born that same night.

STAR STRUCK
July 22, 1934

Judy Garland spent the summer of 1934 in Chicago performing with her family's vaudeville act, the Gumm Sisters. On July 22, 1934, feeling constricted by her workhorse siblings, the 12-year-old singer ditched afternoon rehearsals and walked across town to the Biograph Theater, where the Clark Gable gangster flick *Manhattan Melodrama* was playing. She sat through five showings.

When Garland emerged eight hours later, she spotted a tall, pencil-mustachioed man in a straw hat and swank pinstripe suit, a girl on each arm, exiting along with her. She recognized him but couldn't place him. Assuming he was a movie star, she asked for his autograph. He obliged. Seconds later, he was shot through the head.

That ritzy high roller was John Dillinger—a.k.a. Public Enemy No. 1—and the gunman was a federal agent. Judy had recognized Dillinger from his WANTED posters.

TEAM EFFORT
July 23, 1904

At the 1904 World's Fair in St. Louis, an ice cream vendor named Charles E. Menches claimed to have invented the waffle cone when, having run short on glass bowls, he borrowed a waffle from an adjacent confectioner, folded it, and filled it with two scoops of ice cream.

At the same fair, a vendor named Ernest Hamwi claimed *he* invented the waffle cone when he offered a sample of zalabia, a conical pastry from his native Syria, to a nearby ice creamer.

At the same fair, a Lebanese immigrant named Abe Doumar claimed that it was, in fact, *he* who first struck upon the ingenious notion to marry a conical waffle with a ball of ice cream.

In all, at least eight ice cream and waffle vendors claimed to have invented the waffle cone at the St. Louis World's Fair on July 23, 1904; as soon as the first vendor began selling ice cream in a folded waffle, they all started selling it. To this day, the actual inventor of the waffle cone is unknown.

POE'S PROPHECY
July 24, 1884

On this date, after 19 days at sea, three shipwrecked sailors killed and ate their 19-year-old cabin boy, Richard Parker. The captain recalled:

> *I put my knife [into his neck]. The blood spurted out, and we caught it in the bailer and we drank the blood while it was warm; we then stripped the body, cut it open, and took out his liver and heart, and we ate the liver while it was still warm.*

This tragic account might have been forgotten if not for its eerie coincidence with a tale by Edgar Allan Poe written half a century earlier. In Poe's only novel, *The Narrative of Arthur Gordon Pym* (1838), the four crewmembers of the *Grampus* find themselves adrift without food or water. After two weeks at sea, they draw straws for a cannibalistic sacrifice. The honor falls to a young sailor—one Richard Parker.

Not only do the basic facts of the stories line up—the circumstances of the shipwreck, the number of castaways, the name of the victim—but also the details of the murder and devouring. In Poe's tale:

> *He made no resistance whatever, and was stabbed in the back by Peters, when he fell instantly dead. . . . Let it suffice to say that, having in some measure appeased the raging thirst which consumed us by the blood of the victim . . . we devoured the rest of the body, piecemeal, during the four ever memorable days of the seventeenth, eighteenth, nineteenth, and twentieth of the month.*

PLAGUE OF WORMS
July 25, 1872

During a rainstorm, small animals may be sucked into clouds by whirlwinds and rained back down upon the earth days later like the plague of Egypt. On July 25, 1872, beneath a cloudless sky in Bucharest, Romania, residents went out for an evening stroll. "The gardens were crowded," reported the *Levant Times*. "The ladies were mostly dressed in white low-necked robes." Suddenly, a cloud appeared on the horizon. As it neared, plump, black worms began splattering down on the garden paths, onto dinner plates, through open windows—and down the low-cut eveningwear of the garden walkers.

TO BUILD A WORD
July 26, 1869

King Henry VIII established the Church of Ireland in 1536, six years after his break with the Vatican. Those who supported the new Irish church were called "establishment*arians*," and the movement as a whole was "establishmentarian*ism*."

On July 26, 1869, England passed the Irish Church Act, or *Dis*establishment Bill, disassociating Henry's church from the state. Those who favored the bill were "*dis*establishment," and an individual of such persuasion was a "disestablishment*arian*." The movement as a whole was "disestablishmentarian*ism*."

A movement soon arose against disestablishment. These opponents were termed "*anti*disestablishment," and to refer to one of these individuals one drew on the word "antidisestablishment*arian*." The movement as a whole was called, naturally, "antidisestablishmentarian*ism*."

A piece-by-piece breakdown of this long and mighty word—the longest nontechnical word in the English language—is a study in three centuries of English political history.

THE SLAP HEARD 'ROUND THE WORLD
July 27, 1990

On this day, Hungarian-American B-list actress and socialite Zsa Zsa Gabor—one of the first "famous for being famous" celebrities—arrived at El Segundo Jail to begin a three-day sentence for slapping a Beverly Hills motorcycle cop. The judge might have been more lenient had the 73-year-old socialite not had a prior conviction: Years earlier, she had hit a British constable with her pocketbook.

Gabor clashed constantly with Judge Charles G. Rubin during the trial—she called him "that nasty judge" when he tacked community service onto her sentence, and at one point she stormed out of court and threatened to run away to Europe. Judge Rubin had to halt arguments on one occasion to tell Gabor not to sketch the jury members.

MATCHMAKER, MATCHMAKER
July 28, 1540

Thomas Cromwell, King Henry VIII's right-hand man, was adept at dismantling love—he engineered Henry's divorce from Catherine of Aragon—but he wasn't good at putting it together. In 1539, he arranged Henry's marriage to Anne of Cleves, who supposedly so repulsed the king that he was unable even to consummate the union.

"I see nothing in this woman as men report of her," Henry raged at his henchman, "and I marvel that wise men would make such report as they have done!" When asked how the wedding night went, he told Cromwell—whose credibility as an advisor was now on the wane—"I left her as good a maid as I found her."

While Anne got off with a hasty annulment, Cromwell was not so lucky. He met his death on the chopping block on July 28, 1540, for the high crime of being a terrible cupid.

THE CURSE OF CURZON PLACE
July 29, 1974

Harry Nilsson's two-bedroom flat at 9 Curzon Place, in London's Mayfair, hosted a slew of inebriated couch-crashers in the early 1970s; a five-minute stumble from the Playboy Club, it was the go-to spot for the singer's friends to light up or come down after a heavy night of partying. One of those friends was Cass Elliott, formerly Mama Cass of The Mamas and the Papas. On July 29, 1974, she came back to Nilsson's to sleep after a solo performance at the nearby London Palladium. She never woke up, dying of heart failure at age 32.

Believing the apartment cursed, Nilsson rolled back his open-door policy. When Keith Moon of The Who, a man who had caroused enough in his short life for a thousand people, asked to rent the flat while Nilsson was away on tour in 1978, Nilsson hesitated. It was Pete Townshend, Moon's bandmate, who ultimately convinced him: "Lightning [won't] strike the same place twice," he told Nilsson. Nilsson relented and gave Moon the keys. A month later, Moon died in his sleep in the very same room—in the very same bed—as Mama Cass, and at the same young age of 32.

Nilsson couldn't face returning to the flat. He put it on the market and moved out to Los Angeles, far away from that cursed address.

THE OLDEST OLYMPIAN
July 30, 1932

Until 1952, Olympic medals were awarded in such non-athletic categories as literature, music, sculpture, and city planning. On July 30, 1932, Winslow Homer, the American painter known for his rich seascapes, became the world's oldest Olympian when his watercolor *Casting* was entered into the painting event of the 1932 Summer Games in Los Angeles.

Homer was also deceased at the time, making him not only the oldest Olympic competitor, at 96 years, 157 days, but the only dead one, too.

DORD
July 31, 1931

On this day, a careless dictionary editor at *Merriam-Webster* scrawled an editorial note—"D or d, cont./density"—indicating that the word *density* can be abbreviated as either *D* or *d*. Another careless editor misinterpreted the note, squashed the letters together, and added the nonexistent word *dord* to the next edition of the book.

For five years, sandwiched between *Dorcopsis* and *doré on* page 771 in *Merriam-Webster's New International Dictionary*, *dord* appeared erroneously as another word for *density*.

WHERE WE LAY OUR SCENE
August 1, 1578

Juliet Capulet is the only fictional Shakespearean character whose date of birth is known with absolute precision. In Act 1, Scene 3 of *Romeo and Juliet,* Juliet's nurse reminds Lady Capulet, "On Lammas-eve at night shall she be fourteen. That shall she, marry; I remember it well. 'Tis since the earthquake now eleven years; and she was wean'd." Lammas falls on the first of August, and the quake referred to hit the Dover Strait in 1580. If Juliet is 13 at the time of the play, then she was born on the night of August 1, 1578—a Friday.

Juliet isn't in great company. The only other fictional luminary who shares her birthday is Batman's nemesis, the Joker.

BURY ME NEXT TO BILL
August 2

While mulling a two-pair poker hand of black aces and eights (the "dead man's hand," as it became known), the great American gunslinger Wild Bill Hickock was shot through the back of the head on August 2, 1876. His friend and fellow Wild West legend, Calamity Jane, died of pneumonia on August 2, 1903 (some sources say August 1), following a night of heavy drinking.

Even in her ailing state, Jane didn't fail to notice the extraordinary timing. Her last words were said to be, "It's the 27th anniversary of Bill's death. Bury me next to Bill." They did.

A LESSON IN PERSEVERANCE
August 3, 1970

The record for taking and failing a driving test belongs to Miriam Hargrave of Wakefield, England. After her 31st attempt, she told a newspaper, "I've spent all my savings and my husband has threatened to leave me if I don't give up trying." After her 38th attempt, she said, "I was so confident this time, but it just didn't work." After her 39th, she had to apologize to her driving school: she had just crashed its test vehicle through a red light.

The 62-year-old grandmother finally passed her driving test on August 3, 1970—her 40th try. Ironically, she had spent so much money on driver's ed—$720 on 212 lessons—that she could no longer afford a car.

DRINKING THE STARS
August 4, 1693

Dom Pérignon, a Benedictine monk, supposedly discovered champagne on this day when he dipped into a "botched" batch of red wine for a taste. According to legend, he remarked, "Come quickly! I am drinking the stars!"

The story, sadly, is a myth. If anything, Dom tried to keep bubbles *out* of wine. At the Abbey of Hautvillers where he lived, he was tasked with preventing wine bottles from bursting in the cellar, the result of unwanted carbonation caused by poor storage conditions. As the cellar became too warm, yeast would metabolize excess sugar and re-ferment the wine inside the bottles, producing pressure that caused the glass to shatter. Sparkling wine was a flaw, not a value.

To withstand this fizzy buildup, Dom purportedly introduced thicker glass bottles, stronger corks, and a hemp rope "muselet" to prevent the cork from popping—a prototype of the wire cage used today. Dom didn't invent champagne; it was his greatest nuisance.

ONE GIANT BLUNDER
August 5, 2006

In 1969, we put a man on the moon. Then we lost the video footage.

The Sydney Morning Herald broke the story of NASA's archival mishandling on August 5, 2006, under the headline "One Giant Blunder for Mankind: How NASA Lost Moon Pictures." At some point between 1969 and 2006, the paper claimed, the space agency misplaced approximately 700 boxes of flight tapes—among which was the original high-quality footage of Neil Armstrong's "small step."

"It is feared the magnetic tapes that recorded the first moon walk . . . have gone missing at NASA's Goddard Space Centre in Maryland," read the *Herald* report. "A desperate search has begun amid concerns the tapes will disintegrate to dust before they can be found."

In fact, the moon tapes had neither been lost nor turned to dust. After a three-year search, NASA concluded they had likely been erased and reused some time in the 1980s in an effort to save money on videotapes.

AND ANOTHER ONE
August 6, 1964

On this day, while boring into a Great Basin bristlecone pine to collect a tree-ring sample, a geology student named Donald Rusk Currey got his drill bit stuck. He called a park ranger, who returned with a chainsaw and cut the tree down. Currey retrieved his instrument and his sample and returned to his lab to count the rings.

As he tallied through the night, Currey found himself journeying deeper and deeper into history. His tree-ring count took him past the birth of America, past the dawn of Christianity, past even the pyramids of Egypt. This gnarly, 20-foot-tall pine turned out to be 4,862 years old—just a few years younger than recorded human history.

Currey not only felled the oldest tree ever encountered at the time—he killed the oldest known living organism on Earth.

CHICKEN TREADMILL
August 7, 1906

Before factory farms began cramming chickens into tiny pens with nary enough room to flap around, ranchers made sure their fowl got plenty of exercise. The healthier the chicken, the longer it lived; the longer it lived, the better the egg production.

One method of compelling chickens to hit the gym was to actually build a gym inside the coop. On August 7, 1906, William Jared Manly, of Erie, Pennsylvania, patented a chicken treadmill that chickens could operate on their own. His device utilized a moving platform with a conveyor belt, with a box of bird feed at the far end. In order to eat, chickens had to run faster than the belt.

Sadly, Manly's workout machine never caught on. As farming became industrialized in the twentieth century, ranchers shifted their preference from lean, longer-living chicks to plump, shorter-living ones. The less fit the bird, the plumper it grew; the plumper it grew, the sooner it could be harvested for meat.

THE PASSING OF A GREAT MAN
August 8, 1945

The French flatulist Joseph Pujol—a.k.a. *the Fartiste*—rose to fame for his remarkable ability to pass gas at will, a crude barroom trick that he turned into a high-paying gig at the Moulin Rouge. Upon Joseph's death on August 8, 1945, a Parisian medical school offered his family 25,000 francs to study his rectum. His son rejected the offer, saying, "There are some things in this life which simply must be treated with reverence."

A FLAGRANT EXHIBITION
August 9, 1979

On this day, Eileen Jakes, a local Brighton grandmother, won a concerted campaign to designate Britain's first public nude beach. Her most forthright opponent had been Tory councilor John Blackman, who had a singular way with words.

"I personally have no objection to people showing their breasts and bosoms and general genitalia to each other," said Blackman. "Jolly good luck to them. But for heaven's sake, go somewhere a little more private."

In her effort to persuade Blackman and other legislators, Jakes circulated among the Brighton City Council photographs of herself bathing topless in Spain. Blackman responded with his characteristic eloquence: "A flagrant exhibition of mammary glands," he called it.

PAIN KILLER
August 10, 1897

German chemist Felix Hoffmann joined the Bayer Company in the summer of 1894 as a researcher in the field of painkillers. On August 10, 1897, he synthesized salicylic acid, producing the pharmaceutical known today as *aspirin*. Eleven days later, he acetylated morphine, creating the substance known as *heroin* (which Bayer then marketed as a cough medicine). Inside of two weeks, Hoffman invented one of humanity's most harmless and ubiquitous drugs—as well as its most dangerous and illicit one.

WONDER WOMAN
August 11, 1942

Hedy Lamarr, the actress once known around Hollywood as the "world's most beautiful woman" (and prior to that as the "Ecstasy Lady," for simulating cinema's first on-screen orgasm in the racy 1933 Czech film *Ecstasy*), was also a talented inventor. She holds several patents—one for an improved stoplight, another for an Alka-Seltzer–like carbonation tablet—but her most important one is for a technology that didn't find its market until some 60 years after it was invented. Lamarr's frequency-hopping spread spectrum, which allows radios to communicate in code, is the basis for Wi-Fi.

With America's entry into WWII and her Jewish family in danger back home in Austria, Lamarr lost interest in Hollywood glamour and turned her attention to the war effort. Upon learning that Germany had been jamming Allied radio frequencies and throwing torpedoes off course, Lamarr set out to design an encoding device. On August 11, 1942, Lamarr received U.S. patent number 2292387 for a secret communications technology that allowed radio signals to "hop" between frequencies, thereby avoiding enemy interference.

It wasn't until after Lamarr's death in 2000 that her accomplishment was fully realized. As the digital age exploded, Lamarr's technology found its proper home in Wi-Fi, Bluetooth, and other cell technology, none of which would exist if not for Lamarr. In 2014 she was inducted into the National Inventors Hall of Fame—an honor that may even outshine her star on Hollywood Boulevard.

ON THE ROAD
August 12, 1888

On August 12, 1888, Bertha Benz, wife of automobile inventor Karl Benz, snuck a car out of her husband's workshop in Mannheim, Germany, and drove 66 miles to see her mother. It was the world's first long distance road trip.

Along the way, Bertha hit some snags. When she ran low on fuel, she bought out a chemist's entire stock of ligroin, a petroleum-based mixture sold as a solvent. When she wore out her brake linings in Bauschlott, she had a cobbler fit a new leather pad. She used her metal hatpin to clean out a clogged fuel pipe, and her garter to insulate a frayed ignition wire. When her three-horsepower engine stalled going up a hill, she enlisted the help of two farm boys to push from behind.

Karl Benz had been reluctant to show off his prototypes, hiding them in his shop until they were "perfect." Prior to Bertha's voyage, the Patent Motorwagen No. 3 had only ever been driven a few yards at a time, mostly around the Benz's garage. After the voyage, it was all anyone in southwest Germany could talk about. Bertha was more than a road warrior. She was a clever PR agent.

KING CON
August 13, 1913

According to his autobiography, German circus acrobat Otto Witte once disguised himself as an Albanian prince and tricked the royal household into crowning him King of Albania for five days.

The mustachioed performer noticed his resemblance to Prince Halim Eddine, the sultan's estranged nephew, in an article announcing Albania's independence from the Ottoman Empire. The paper invited Prince Eddine home to claim the throne, so Witte donned a fez and fancy regalia and rode into town to take what was unrightfully his.

He was coronated on August 13, 1913, in Durrës, and immediately began exploring the privileges of the position: he declared war on Montenegro, set all prisoners in his kingdom free, and indulged in his royal harem. When cables arrived from the actual Prince Eddine five days later, King Otto fled, taking a large portion of the royal treasury with him.

Sadly—but not surprisingly—no evidence exists of the episode outside of Witte's autobiography. (Witte was a known liar and had spun many other outsized tales of similar brushes with royalty. He once claimed he served as chief of an African Pygmy tribe, and on another occasion had eloped with the daughter of Ethiopia's emperor.) Nevertheless, Witte swore by his tale, and for the rest of his life insisted on being addressed by his former title. The German government eventually allowed "Former King of Albania" on his identity card, and Witte had the words engraved on his tombstone in Ohlsdorf Cemetery, in Germany. He died on August 13, 1958, exactly 45 years after his alleged coronation.

DON'T BE CRUEL
August 14, 1956

On this day, Bob Rickman, a Washington, D.C., disc jockey and Elvis Presley acolyte, formed the Society for the Prevention of Cruelty to Elvis Presley, a group committed to stopping unfair press coverage of the singer.

When Elvis first hit it big in 1956, he had few friends in the press. Conservative reporters denounced him as an oversexed hedonist, while more liberal writers considered him a dimwitted country bumpkin. To bolster the "Hillbilly Elvis" image, some newspapers transcribed his speech phonetically to exaggerate his inarticulateness. The following interview appeared in the *Dayton Daily News* in the spring of 1956:

Q: What do you have that sends girls?

A: Ah cain't answer that. An' anyhow, what difference it make? Long as they come see me. Ah love every one of 'em.

Q: Do you think you'll make it in the movies?

A: That's what Ah wanta be, an actor. . . . Movies you don't work alla time. An' make big money. That's for me. Travelin' alla time, Ah don't get no sleep. Ah'm tard.

Rickman's activism may have worked: By 1957 Elvis was the darling of the media—his lack of sophistication now a "lack of pretention," his hillbilly speech now "pleasantly tinged with a southern drawl." Despite its bias against the gee-tar–strumming country boy, the press couldn't help falling in love with him.

NO RSVP NECESSARY
August 15, 2004

To celebrate his ascension to Prince Regent, Alois of Liechtenstein invited all 34,600 Liechtenstein residents to a garden party at his house to meet, mingle, and imbibe with the royal family. So popular was the reception that the prince now holds a public party at his castle every year on August 15.

STRING THEORY
August 16, 2008

Jamaican sprinter Usain Bolt, the fastest human ever recorded as of this book's publication, set a world record in the 100-meter final at the Beijing Olympics with his left shoelace untied.

Shoelaces come undone by the force of impact of the foot hitting the ground, and the chances of mishap are increased by an uneven stride. Bolt's scoliosis—and the fact that his right leg is half an inch shorter than his left—could have been responsible for the lace's unraveling.

SLAPHAPPY
August 17, 1957

Philadelphia Phillies centerfielder Richie Ashburn could foul pitches off at will, but one day he got a little too slaphappy. During a game against the New York Giants on August 17, 1957, Ashburn slapped a foul ball that struck a fan, Alice Roth, squarely in the face, breaking her nose. As medics carried her away on a stretcher, Ashburn hit the next pitch foul and socked Roth again, this time in her leg.

Roth happened to be the wife of Earl Roth, the sports editor of the *Philadelphia Bulletin*. When Ashburn became eligible for the Hall of Fame years later (a vote cast by sportswriters around the country), the *Bulletin* voted against him 15 years in a row.

MEMORY BUILDER
August 18, 1885

On this day, Mark Twain patented *"Mark Twain's Memory Builder: A Game for Acquiring and Retaining All Sorts of Facts and Dates."* (Like this one.)

Twain's notion of an "important" fact is a bit musty: "The most conspicuous landmarks in history," he writes in the instruction manual, "are the accessions of kings," followed by battles, and then by "minor events." A player who correctly answers that James I ascended the English throne in 1603, for example, earns 10 points. Remembering that the Battle of Waterloo took place in 1815 nets a player 5 points. For knowing that the Declaration of Independence was signed in 1776—in Twain's eyes a "minor event," of mere local interest—a player is rewarded 1 point.

SIGN STEALER
August 19, 1996

On his 64th birthday, Banharn Silpa-archa, the Prime Minister of Thailand, stood accused of fraud by his Parliament. His critics claimed that his birthday was actually in July—but that he changed it to August 19 on the advice of a fortuneteller who assured him the corresponding zodiac sign would be auspicious for a political career.

Others said the real reason for the date change is that he wanted to share a birthday with then–U.S. President Bill Clinton.

This, and many other more serious allegations of fraud, forced Banharn Silpa-archa's resignation later that year.

POWER HUNGRY
August 20, 1672

The year 1672 is known in Dutch history as the *rampjaar,* or "disaster year." In March, England attacked an off-guard Dutch trade fleet, provoking it into a bloody two-day battle resulting in heavy Dutch casualties. In April, France and Germany declared war on Holland. In June, Louis XIV's army assaulted Holland from the south, the Bishopric of Münster attacked from the east, and lower and middle-class Dutch citizens rebelled against their government from within. A phrase was coined to describe the state of Holland in 1672: *"Het volk redeloos, de regering radeloos, en het land reddeloos"*—"The people were irrational, the government desperate, and the country irretrievable."

In the hysteria of the disasters, William III of Orange, a contender for the Dutch premiership, overthrew Prime Minister Johan de Witt and tossed his brother, Cornelis de Witt, into The Hague as a traitor. When Johan went to visit Cornelis on August 20, an enraged mob stormed the prison, murdered their former prime minister and his brother, and ate them.

Though William denied that he ordered the killings, his actions afterward were suspect. He protected the cannibals from prosecution and even rewarded some with government appointments.

A GOOD DAY FOR AN ART HEIST
August 21

On the morning of August 21, 1911, an out-of-work Italian carpenter, dressed as a repairman, casually removed the *Mona Lisa* from a gallery wall in the Louvre and walked out with it tucked under his smock. Exactly 50 years later, on August 21, 1961, a man climbed into London's National Gallery through a restroom window, nicked Francisco Goya's *Portrait of the Duke of Wellington*, and escaped the way he had come in (a baffling accomplishment considering the man was in his 60s and weighed 250 pounds). Exactly 49 years after that, on August 21, 2010, thieves entered a museum in Cairo and sliced Vincent van Gogh's *Poppy Flowers* out of its frame with box cutters. They, too, escaped with ease.

Honorable mention: On August 22, 2004, two thieves made off with Edvard Munch's *The Scream* and *Madonna* from the Munch Museum. The previous day had been stormy in Oslo—chalk that one up to a rain check?

THE POP
August 22, 1978

In the dogma of the Catholic Church, the Pope is considered infallible—but God save him from the errors of newspaper columnists. On page 19 of the August 22, 1978, edition of the London *Times*, 97 misprints appeared in a single 5 1/2-inch column. Most of the typos concerned Pope Paul VI, who was referred to throughout as "the Pop."

THE OTHER MICHAEL JACKSON
August 23, 1978

For about eight weeks in 1978, two songs named "Blame It on the Boogie" occupied the UK Singles Chart, each performed by different people named Michael Jackson.

As one Michael Jackson soared to fame in the 1970s with the family music group The Jacksons (formerly the Jackson 5), another Michael Jackson—a 30-year-old disco singer from Yorkshire, England—was trying to score a hit across the pond. Though he'd had minor success with a few middling records, his self-penned track "Blame It On The Boogie" was expected to be his breakthrough. He recorded it in 1977, but in the time between its recording and release his publisher sold it, without the singer's knowledge, to The Jacksons' management team. On August 23, 1978, a week after the British Michael Jackson released his record, The Jacksons dropped their version as an advance single from their hotly anticipated album *Destiny*. The tracks jockeyed for chart position, but it was clear which would win. The Jacksons' song became an anthem of the disco era. The Brit's stalled at number 15.

His career never recovered, but Michael from Yorkshire—or Mick, as he started calling himself afterward—made out just fine in the end. His songwriting credit keeps the checks pouring in and even helped to fund "Battle of the Boogie," his son's 2010 documentary about the 1978 incident.

MAKE IT RAIN
August 24, 1967

Abbie Hoffman, the rabble-rousing cofounder of the Yippies, was known for his large-scale anarchist publicity stunts. His first act of political theater occurred on August 24, 1967, when he and 15 radical friends took a tour of the New York Stock Exchange. As the tour ended, the Yippies took out wads of dollar bills and tossed them off a balcony overlooking the trading floor. Three hundred green banknotes fluttered down over the exchange and trading was halted for six minutes as brokers scrambled for the bills.

Two weeks after Hoffman's political stunt, the NYSE spent twenty thousand dollars to enclose the gallery with bulletproof glass.

VAMPIRES ON THE MOON
August 25, 1835

On this day, an article appeared in the New York *Sun* announcing that scientists had discovered vampires on the moon—along with bison, goats, beavers, and unicorns.

"Their attitude in walking was both erect and dignified. . . ." wrote the paper of these winged lunar man-bats. "They averaged four feet in height, were covered, except on the face, with short and flossy copper-colored hair, and had wings composed of a thin membrane, without hair, lying snugly upon their backs, from the top of their shoulders to the calves of their legs."

The findings had been made with the aid of "an immense telescope of an entirely new principle" that could supposedly reduce the sight-distance to the lunar surface to 80 yards. Newspapers across the country reprinted the story and scientists debated the findings for weeks. The *Sun*'s circulation jumped—and stayed high even after the author admitted he'd made up the whole thing.

THE BANTING DIET
August 26, 1862

Before Robert Atkins came along, there was William Banting, the original low-carb weight loss guru. On August 26, 1862, after years of struggle with joint pain and shortness of breath, the overweight London funeral director abruptly cut out potatoes, bread, sugar, milk, and beer and began a love affair with meats and vegetables. Two weeks later, he was down two pounds. By Christmas, he had dropped 16 more. And so on did the fat shed until the following September, when Banting weighed in at 156 pounds—46 pounds lighter than when he set out.

After publicizing the diet in his pamphlet "A Letter on Corpulence," Banting became history's first weight loss celebrity. His name became synonymous with slimming down, and the verb *bant* entered the Oxford English Dictionary as another word for *diet*. "Do you bant?" was a common query among fitness enthusiasts until the 1960s, when the slang fell out of favor.

Banting also coined the diet ad clichés familiar to us today: He conceived the "before-and-after photo" (even if he lacked the foresight to take the "before" pic; he was already well into the diet when it occurred to him) and would pose for family and friends wearing his old clothing, thumbing out his former waistband like a TV diet spokesperson.

THE 38-MINUTE WAR
August 27, 1896

The shortest war in recorded history occurred on August 27, 1896, between the British Empire and the African island state of Zanzibar. It lasted 38 minutes.

The conflict began with the death of Hamad bin Thuwaini, the pro-British sultan of Zanzibar, on August 25, and the forceful seizure of power by his anti-British cousin Khalid bin Barghash. Khalid's rise to power violated an 1886 treaty with Britain promising the Empire (under whose protectorate Zanzibar fell at the time) the authority to sign off on any Zanzibari leader. Britain sent an ultimatum to the new sultan: he had until 9 a.m. on the 27th to step down.

One hour before the ultimatum expired, Sultan Khalid dispatched a reply to the British consul: "We have no intention of hauling down our flag, and we do not believe you would open fire on us." Basil Cave, a British diplomat to Zanzibar, responded, "We do not want to open fire, but unless you do as you are told we shall certainly do so." At 8:55 a.m., having received no further reply, the British warship *St George* hoisted the signal to prepare for action.

At 9:02, three British warships bombarded Zanzibar Palace, setting it on fire and destroying most of Khalid's artillery. By 9:40, British troops had stormed the beach, the sultan's flag had been removed, and all gunfire had ceased. The war was over.

HONORARY BLOCKHEAD
August 28, 1938

On this day, Charlie McCarthy, the original insult comic puppet, received an honorary degree from Northwestern University. The foul-mouthed ventriloquist dummy got his Master's degree in the field of "Innuendo and the Snappy Comeback."

One Chicago journalist wrote:

> *There may be academic reactionaries who will protest that the university, in bestowing cap and gown upon a piece of fence post, is donning the cap and bells of the jester it honors. But we see nothing incongruous in the ceremony. Certainly it will not be the first time that a blockhead has received a university degree.*

FROM AA TO LSD
August 29, 1956

In the winter of 1934, a New York stock speculator and alcoholic named Bill Wilson was being treated at a Manhattan hospital for delirium tremens—a.k.a. alcohol withdrawal—when suddenly he cried out, "I'll do anything! Anything at all! If there be a God, let him show himself!" As the legend goes, Wilson saw a white light, heard the sound of rushing wind, and felt a sense of peace. That was it. He never drank again.

The next year Wilson and physician Bob Smith founded Alcoholics Anonymous, a recovery program to help addicts overcome addiction through spiritual breakthrough. Over the next 20 years, thousands of alcoholics found sobriety using Wilson's methods—yet even the most dedicated program members often fell short of the full-blown religious epiphany that Wilson encouraged (the final step in the "Twelve-step Program"). By the 1950s, Wilson began looking for a shortcut.

Psychotherapy was fixated at the time on the study of a new chemical, lysergic acid diethylamide—a.k.a. LSD, or "acid"—which experiments had shown to be useful in helping patients clear repressed subconscious blockages. On August 29, 1956, Wilson decided to test it for himself. The AA founder dropped acid with Aldous Huxley and experienced something he hadn't felt since that night on his hospital bed. He immediately made plans to incorporate LSD into addiction recovery.

Wilson formed an LSD research group in New York, and began regularly ingesting the chemical in supervised self-experiments. But as word of Wilson's activities spread among AA, a major scandal arose. Pressured to resign, Wilson left AA and continued his LSD experiments alone, detached from the organization he had breathed life into two decades earlier.

A PECULIAR RACE
August 30, 1904

The Olympic marathon in St. Louis on this day might have been the most unusual Olympic event ever. The first-place finisher was Frederick Lorz, an American runner who had surreptitiously hitched to the finish line in a car. When he was found out, he gave up his gold medal to second-place Thomas Hicks, who was so doped up on brandy and strychnine sulfate (a rat poison that stimulates the nervous system in small doses, enhancing athletic performance) that he could barely stand for the awards ceremony. Fourth place went to Andarín Carvajal, the Cuban-born favorite, who had stopped along the way to eat from an apple tree, got stomach cramps, and took a nap mid-race.

A FOOL'S GOLD
August 31, 1578

On this day, Sir Martin Frobisher, an English privateer, set out on his return to Britain loaded with 1,400 tons of what he thought was gold, mined from Baffin Island in northeastern Canada. After years of smelting, it proved to be worthless iron pyrite. Frobisher's "gold" was later used to make road gravel in England.

REVIEW OF MYSELF
September 1, 1855

On this day, Walt Whitman penned an anonymous rave review of his own book, the recently published poetry collection *Leaves of Grass*. "His scope of life is the amplest of any yet in philosophy," he wrote of himself in the *United States Review*. ". . . He is the largest lover and sympathizer that has appeared in literature."

Whitman's self-fawning was exposed when readers pointed out stylistic similarities between his poems and his reviews. His exuberant, iambic pronouncement of himself as "An American Bard at last!" was probably what did him in.

OH, CANADA
September 2, 2013

At a freshman sex education program at the University of New Brunswick, volunteers handed out free condoms stapled to a note endorsing sexual consent. "Consent is sexy," read the pink and purple card stock note. The condoms were recalled when someone noticed the staples had punctured holes in the latex.

IS KETCHUP A VEGETABLE?
September 3, 1981

In order to satisfy nutritional requirements for school lunches, the U.S. Food and Nutrition service announced on this day that it would count condiments as vegetables.

According to the new government guidelines, "a condiment such as pickle relish" could now be considered a serving of cucumber, and "one tablespoon of tomato paste could be credited as 1/4 cup single-strength tomato juice." Donuts could also, in theory, be counted as bread.

Facing severe public backlash, U.S. President Ronald Reagan withdrew the nutritional regulations before the end of the month. But not everyone ceded defeat. James Johnson, aide to the U.S. Agriculture secretary, said, "There was a great misunderstanding in the land as to how these regulations are viewed. I think it would be a mistake to say that ketchup *per se* was classified as a vegetable. . . . Ketchup in combination with other things was classified as a vegetable."

"What other things?" asked a reporter.

"French fries or hamburgers," Johnson replied.

SUGAR PLUM 4 LIFE
September 4, 1986

Behind Tupac Shakur's hard exterior was a soft spot for ballet. On September 4, 1986, the 15-year-old future rapper entered the prestigious Baltimore School for the Arts to study dancing and acting. At BSA, he played the lead in Shakespeare's *Othello*, won a few poetry competitions, and filmed a hip-hop video with his classmate Jada Pinkett. (By chance, they lip-synced to a song by Pinkett's future husband, Will Smith.)

The highlight of Tupac's high school days, however, was not miming to the Fresh Prince but arabesquing to Tchaikovsky. In his senior year, Tupac "Thug 4 Life" Shakur donned silver tights and ballet slippers to play the Mouse King in *The Nutcracker*.

THE LONGEST SONG IN THE WORLD
September 5, 2640

John Cage wrote "As Slow as Possible" without indicating a time signature, daring musicians to interpret the title as they see fit.

A friendly competition arose among avant-gardists and performance artists to out-slow each other. The first performance lasted 29 minutes, the next lasted 71 minutes. In February 2009, music professor Diane Luchese performed from 8:45 a.m. to 11:41 p.m. at a concert hall at Towson University in Maryland. At the ARTSaha! music festival in Omaha, Nebraska, in 2008, Joe Drew stretched the composition over 24 hours.

The most extreme interpretation has been playing on a wooden organ at St. Burchardi church in Halberstadt, Germany, since 2001—and will still be going long after we're gone. Using weights to hold down the pedals and a bellows to feed the pipes, the organ rendition is currently playing at an average rate of one note per year and isn't expected to end until September 5, 2640.

TELL TALE
September 6, 1951

Over the centuries, many a reckless marksman has attempted the William Tell feat of sniping an apple from atop someone's head. One of the most tragic cases was that of the Beat writer William S. Burroughs and his wife, Joan Vollmer. During a party on September 6, 1951, Burroughs took out a pistol and announced to his fellow revelers, "It's time for our William Tell act!" Joan then placed an apple atop her head. Burroughs aimed, fired, and accidentally shot Vollmer, killing her on the spot.

MUSEUM DESPOILERS
September 7, 1911

Two weeks after a thief stole the *Mona Lisa* from the Louvre, Paris police arrested their top suspect—the French poet Guillaume Apollinaire. Under questioning, Apollinaire accidentally implicated his friend, an unknown Spanish artist named Pablo Picasso, and the two were briefly detained as suspected leaders of—in the words of the Police Nationale—"an international gang come to France to despoil our museums."

During Apollinaire's interrogation, Paris Magistrate Henri Drioux raised an incident from the poet's past that supposedly spoke to his tendency for theft. The following exchange occurred:

> *Drioux: I have a letter here from someone who says that you borrowed two books from him, and that one of them, La Cité Gauloise, you never returned.*
>
> *Apollinaire: I imagine his reason for lending them to me was that I might read them. I haven't read them yet. I will return them to him as soon as I can.*

Apollinaire and Picasso were both released within a week. The real thief was caught in Italy in 1913.

AND ON THIS BOAT HE HAD A . . .
September 8, 1827

On this day, in the first recorded Niagara Falls tourist stunt, three hotel owners sailed a small schooner over the 180-foot precipice carrying two bears, two raccoons, a buffalo, a dog, and a goose. A crowd of 10,000 came out to watch the stunt, and local bars on both sides of the falls ran out of booze. Only the goose and the bears survived.

OMG
September 9, 1917

Sir Winston Churchill, one of the most eloquent orators in British history, played an unwitting role in shaping the texting vernacular of today's teenagers. In a letter to Churchill dated September 9, 1917, the Admiral of the British Navy coined the acronym OMG:

"I hear that a new order of Knighthood is on the tapis—
O.M.G. (Oh! My God!)—Shower it on the Admiralty!!"

THE FRAUD OF POYAIS
September 10, 1822

On this day, 70 European émigrés boarded a ship for Poyais, a nonexistent country made up by a Scottish conman named Gregor MacGregor.

Beginning in 1821, MacGregor swindled hundreds of British investors into buying government bonds and land certificates to his imaginary state. He designed a flag and a coat of arms, printed up Poyaisan bank notes, and even published a 385-page guidebook—*Sketch of the Mosquito Shore, Including the Territory of Poyais*—describing the republic as a flourishing 8-million acre utopia in Central America teeming with people, theaters, opera houses, cathedrals, mansions, boulevards, and a royal palace. In the rivers of Poyais, MacGregor claimed, one could rake up "globules of pure gold" with little effort.

Following MacGregor's crude sailing map, the unwitting colonists arrived on a coast near Honduras after eight weeks at sea to find an untouched, inhospitable jungle. Lacking the provisions to return home, they were forced to hunt and forage through the winter. In the spring, a passing schooner spotted them and took them to British Honduras, where they sent word home about MacGregor's scam. By the time the message reached London, MacGregor had already fled to Paris.

MacGregor tried the same scheme in France a few years later, but French authorities were wise to his game. They caught the con artist selling fake land certificates and threw him in prison.

THE BIG SLEEP
September 11, 2001

On the night of September 10, 2001, Michael Jackson, a chronic insomniac, tossed and turned for hours before finally falling asleep around 4 a.m. When he awoke later that morning, he had missed a meeting scheduled in the World Trade Center. "We were terrified when the towers fell," his brother Jermaine recalled. "We knew Michael was due there. But mom said he was fine. He missed his meetings."

The very thing that saved the King of Pop on 9/11 killed him eight years later. Jackson died in 2009 from an overdose of sedatives prescribed to combat insomnia.

A SPECIAL PARDON
September 12, 1379

On this day, Philip the Bold, the Duke of Burgundy, pardoned two herds of swine that had been sentenced to death as accomplices in the trampling of a pig herder by three sows.

The herder, a man named Perrinot, had been tending to the village pigs when three sows rushed him. After rounding up the attackers, authorities detained two nearby herds on suspicion of conspiracy. The owner of the alleged conspirators petitioned Philip to show mercy, and Philip obliged. "[We must] content ourselves with making an example of three or four of these pigs and to liberate the remainder," said the duke. "Bowing to his request, we grant and approve a special pardon."

GOOD VIBRATIONS
September 13, 2011

In a bizarre attempt to improve cell phone accessibility, Nokia filed a patent on this day for a vibrating tattoo that alerts users when their cell phone rings. The tattoo uses magnetized ink that can be synced up, Bluetooth-style, to one's cell phone. When a call comes in, the phone emits a magnetic wave that triggers a tactile response on the user's skin.

The technology would also allow users to customize their contacts—two long buzzes for Grandma, staccato for that special someone—and receive signals from laptops and game consoles.

PARTY LIKE IT'S 1787
September 14, 1787

On this day, at an epic farewell bash for George Washington at Philadelphia's City Tavern, 55 revelers racked up a tab for:

> 60 bottles of Bordeaux
> 54 bottles of Madeira wine
> 34 bottles of beer
> 8 bottles of whiskey
> 8 bottles of cider
> 7 large bowls of punch
> and damages for an unspecified number of broken tumblers and wine glasses.

OFF-KEY
September 15, 2016

In the hustle and bustle of election campaigning, U.S. presidential candidates don't always have time to vet their song choices (or don't care if the use holds up to scrutiny). When Ronald Reagan ran for reelection in 1984, he picked Bruce Springsteen's "Born in the U.S.A." for his campaign theme, not realizing that the fist-pumping, patriotic anthem is actually an indictment of the U.S. government. When Rudy Giuliani ran for president in 2008, he used The Clash's "Rudie Can't Fail," a defense of youthful recklessness at odds with his conservative politics. But it's Hillary Clinton's innocently insensitive snafu at a political rally on September 15, 2016, that takes the cake for awkward electoral soundtracks. In her first campaign stop after a debilitating bout of pneumonia, Clinton walked onstage in Greensboro, North Carolina, to James Brown's "I Feel Good." Brown died of pneumonia in 2006.

WHAT FUN IT IS TO RIDE
September 16, 1857

On this day, American songwriter James Lord Pierpont copyrighted "One Horse Open Sleigh"—better known today as "Jingle Bells"—an ode to the New England winter sport of horse-and-sleigh drag racing that used to occur on Salem Street, in Pierpont's home of Medford, Massachusetts. His original lyrics capture the spirit of these cutthroat, alcohol-fueled contests:

The horse was lean and lank
Misfortune seemed his lot
He got into a drifted bank
And then we got upsot . . .

A gent was riding by
In a one-horse open sleigh,
He laughed as there I sprawling lie,
But quickly drove away.

Now the ground is white
Go it while you're young,
Take the girls tonight
and sing this sleighing song.

Considered racy for its time, this speedster's anthem became a popular regional drinking song. It soon overtook Pierpont's previous success, "The Returned Californian," a song about how he lost all his money in the California Gold Rush and then tried to ditch his creditors. Pierpont followed up these sprightly tunes by writing battle songs for the Confederacy.

SPEED DEMON
September 17, 1955

James Dean was a speed demon. In April 1954, after landing his first film role in *East of Eden,* Dean purchased a used 1953 MGTD, a popular English racing car with an inline 4-cylinder engine capable of speeds up to 100 MPH (rare at the time). A few months later he traded it up for a lightweight Porsche Super Speedster that eclipsed the century-mark with a tap of the foot. Dean finished second in his first auto race, the 1955 Palm Springs Road Races, and was officially hooked: for the rest of his short life, Dean got his kicks racing.

His image as a fast-driving bad boy started to grow. On September 17, 1955, on the advice of a wary publicist, Dean filmed a public service announcement for the National Safety Council cautioning youngsters against speeding on highways. "Do you have any special advice for the young people that drive?" asks an interviewer. "Take it easy driving," Dean replies. Then, weaving off-script with a wry smirk, he adlibs a line that would prove morbidly ironic: "The life you might save might be mine."

Dean was killed 13 days later when another car turned into his path while driving on a California highway. Though witnesses claim he wasn't speeding at the time, Dean's behavior that day may suggest otherwise: Two hours before the crash, he received a ticket for going 65 in a 55-mph zone.

TAKE MY CHIROPRACTOR, PLEASE
September 18, 1895

In the early days of chiropractic therapy, the practice was imbued with magic and mysticism and purported to cure anything from diseases to rashes to depression. Its founder, Daniel David Palmer, claimed he invented it when he cured a man of deafness by slapping his back.

The alleged slap occurred on September 18, 1895, when Palmer's friend, Harvey Lillard, told a particularly uproarious joke. Palmer supposedly laughed so hard at the punch line that he slapped Lillard on the back, thereby curing his friend's partial hearing problem. And so chiropractic medicine was born.

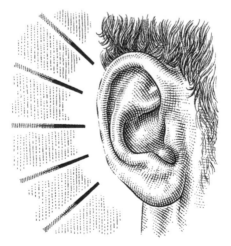

A DUCK, A SHEEP, AND A ROOSTER
WALK INTO A HOT-AIR BALLOON
September 19, 1783

When French inventors Joseph-Michel and Jacques-Étienne Montgolfier announced a public demonstration of the world's first flying machine, King Louis XVI suggested, in typically sadistic fashion, to load it with prisoners and launch them irretrievably into the heavens. The Montgolfier brothers had a kinder idea: rather than expose humans to the unknown hazards of tropospheric flight, they would run a test with a trio of barnyard animals.

In the early afternoon of September 19, 1783, before a crowd of 130,000 outside the royal palace at Versailles, the Montgolfiers placed a duck, a sheep, and a rooster into a wicker basket. A drum roll sounded, the men lit their contraption, and the world's first living aeronauts wobbled high over the palace in their silk blue balloon. The show didn't last long. A northerly gust soon came along and pushed the hot-air balloon toward the woods of Vaucresson, two miles away, where it landed safely eight minutes later.

"It was judged that [the animals] had not suffered," read a later press account, "but they were, to say the least, much astonished."

THE BATTLE OF THE SEXES
September 20, 1973

On September 20, 1973, 55-year-old retired tennis champ Bobby Riggs faced off against 29-year-old Billie Jean King, the top female player in the world at the time, in a nationally televised publicity stunt dubbed the "Battle of the Sexes." In the lead-up, Riggs taunted King with numerous chauvinistic comments, including, "The best way to handle women is to keep them pregnant and barefoot," and "Women play about 25 percent as good as men, so they should get about 25 percent of the money men get." King called him a creep and a pig.

The day of the match, King entered the court Cleopatra-style, in a golden chariot hoisted by four toga-wearing muscle men. Riggs followed in a rickshaw drawn by scantily clad women whom he called "Bobby's bosom buddies." Riggs presented King with a gift: a giant Sugar Daddy lollipop. She, in turn, gave him a squealing baby pig, a symbol of his misogyny. With 90 million people watching, King won the match 6–4, 6–3, and 6–3. Riggs was shattered and reportedly locked himself in his hotel room for hours.

GOING ONCE, GOING TWICE . . .
September 21, 1915

On this day, Cecil Chubb's wife sent him to an auction to buy a set of dining room chairs. He walked away the proud owner of Stonehenge.

The 39-year-old millionaire lawyer won the deed to the ancient monument with a bid of £6,600, at an auction in Salisbury, England. When he told his wife, she was not impressed. Stonehenge then was a weathered, overgrown acre of chalky Wiltshire land, inlaid with some old and unsightly rocks. You couldn't build anything on it. You couldn't entertain dinner guests on it. (The second-highest bidder planned to graze sheep on it.) Few in England cared that it was constructed on a cosmic configuration, aligned to the sunset of the winter solstice and the sunrise of the summer solstice, or that the Druids might have built it for sacrifices and burials, or that the 25-ton stones were sourced from a bluestone quarry some 200 miles away without aid of the wheel. Finding no purpose with it, Chubb donated it to the British government in 1918. Since then it has become one of Britain's most visited historical landmarks.

HAMMER TIME
September 22, 1986

For all of his success in business, Armand Hammer was known in the public mind for a fluke of nomenclature: he shared a name with one of America's leading cleaning supply brands.

Hammer, an industrialist and philanthropist once described by Bob Hope as the "epitome of success," got asked so often about his association with Arm & Hammer that he once offered to buy it. The owners didn't want to sell, so Hammer found a different way in. On September 22, 1986, Hammer's Occidental Petroleum Corporation purchased a five-percent stake in Church & Dwight, a manufacturer of household products. Hammer joined its Board of Directors and took part-ownership of all its products—including a certain brand of baking soda cleanser. At the age of 88, after decades of being dogged by his namesake, Armand Hammer became a part owner of Arm & Hammer.

RESPAWN
September 23, 1889

Nintendo has had a long, strange journey to the top of the video game kingdom. The company that revolutionized gaming in the 1980s with *Donkey Kong* and *Super Mario Bros.* began life on September 23, 1889, as a seller of hand-drawn *hanafuda* playing cards, a popular recreation in Japan similar to a western-style 52-card deck. Before switching to video games in 1972, Nintendo also sold instant rice and remote-controlled vacuum cleaners, and operated a "love hotel" chain that rented rooms by the hour.

HIGH STAKES
September 24, 1765

A splendid time was had by all when, on this day, according to *Lloyd's Evening Post*:

> *A cricket match was played at Upham, Hants, by eleven married against eleven maiden women, for a large plumb-cake [sic], a barrel of ale, and regale of tea, which were won by the latter. After the diversion the company met and drank tea, spent the evening together, and concluded it with a ball.*

Exactly 79 years later, on September 24, 1844, the first official international sporting event took place when the Canadian and American cricket teams faced off at St. George's Cricket Club in New York City. Canada beat the United States by 23 runs. Sadly, there was no plum cake in the stakes.

SNARK MARK
September 25, 1887

In his 1887 essay "For Brevity and Clarity," American satirist Ambrose Bierce proposed an early emoticon called a *snigger point:* "It is written thus ◡ and represents, as nearly as may be, a smiling mouth."

It was meant to be a condescending sneer at the end of a snide remark—a sarcasm indicator rather than an expression of actual happiness. In his example, Bierce couldn't help sneaking in a jab at his journalistic foe, Edward Bok:

> *[The snigger point] is to be appended, with the full stop, to every jocular or ironical sentence; or, without the stop, to every jocular or ironical clause of a sentence otherwise serious—thus: "Mr. Edward Bok is the noblest work of God ◡ ."*

STILL GOT IT
September 26, 1976

Ramses II was the most powerful pharaoh of the Egyptian empire. He ruled for nearly 70 years, built the Temples at Abu Simbel, and is believed to be the pharaoh who wouldn't let Moses's people go. Some three millennia after his death, he was still afforded all the respect and deference of a great sovereign. When his mummified body was flown from Cairo to Paris on September 26, 1976, for fungoid restoration treatment, it was received at Le Bourget Airport with full military honors. The Egyptian embassy even issued Ramses a special passport for the journey. Under "Occupation," it read: "King (deceased)."

LIFE AND LIMB
September 27, 1842

During the Pastry War of 1838—a four-month skirmish between Mexico and France sparked by an unpaid bakery debt—Mexican General Antonio López de Santa Anna lost his leg in battle.

The General sent orders to the Archbishop of Mexico to make preparations for his limb's ceremonial burial. The Archbishop objected. "There is no precedent for religious services over a leg," he protested. ". . . It is not to be thought of." "Let us establish a precedent in that case, Your Reverence," the General insisted. "Mine was a Christian leg; it deserves a Christian burial. So mote it be."

And so on September 27, 1842, General Santa Anna had his detached appendage buried in Santa Paula cemetery with full military honors, in a ceremony that included prayers, choir singing, artillery salvos, and a flowery eulogy recited in honor of the defunct limb. The leg was then placed inside a crystal case and buried beneath an ornate monument.

The leg was gone, but not forgotten; Santa Anna made sure of that. For years, the Mexican General would show up to parades waving around his cork prosthetic to show that he'd given limb, if not life, for his beloved country.

BAD HAIR DAY
September 28, 1567

On this day, Hans Steininger, the chief magistrate of Braunau, Austria, died by tripping over his own beard.

Hans normally kept his four-foot-long mane rolled up in a leather pouch. But when a fire broke out in Braunau, he was caught with his tresses unfurled, and he tripped on them trying to escape, dying either from a broken neck or exposure to the flames.

GREAT BALLS OF GUNFIRE
September 29, 1976

On this day, Jerry Lee Lewis, one of rock-and-roll's first great wild men, shot his bass player Norman Owens in the chest while attempting to snipe a soda bottle with a .357 magnum. Lewis was arrested and charged with shooting a firearm within the city limits.

A prolific drinker, Lewis was arrested again two months later for driving his Rolls Royce into a ditch, and again the very next night outside the gates of Graceland for waving around a .38 derringer and demanding to see Elvis. Strangely enough, Lewis got his nickname "The Killer" for his vigorous piano playing.

MESSAGE IN A BOTTLE
September 30, 1826

A man walking along the Bajan coast on this day found a message in a bottle, wedged in the sand:

> *The ship the Kent, Indiaman, is on fire. Elizabeth, Joanna, and myself commit our spirits into the hands of our blessed Redeemer; His grace enables us to be quite composed in the awful prospect of entering eternity. Dun. MacGregor. 1st of March, 1825. Bay of Biscay.*

By coincidence, the letter's author showed up on the Bajan shore a month later. Duncan MacGregor and his family had been miraculously rescued from the blaze moments after tossing the message into the sea. Duncan returned to seafaring, rose to become Lieutenant Colonel of the 93rd Highlanders, and in October 1826 found his regiment stationed on that same beach in Barbados where his bottle had drifted—three thousand miles from where the *Kent* went down.

A LUCKY GRAB
October 1, 1620

His name may not be common knowledge, but few people have left a greater imprint on American history than John Howland. On October 1, 1620, the 29-year-old *Mayflower* passenger was washed overboard during a violent storm and left for dead. As his shipmates pressed on, Howland managed to snag a trailing halyard and pull himself back on board. He went on to have 10 children and 88 grandchildren, and became the direct ancestor of nearly two million modern Americans, including Humphrey Bogart, the Roosevelts, the two Presidents Bush, Sarah Palin, the Baldwin brothers, Chevy Chase, Ralph Waldo Emerson, and Mormon church founder Joseph Smith.

UP HIGH
October 2, 1977

On this final day of the regular baseball season, in Los Angeles, Dodgers outfielder Dusty Baker crushed a homerun. As he rounded third base, teammate Glenn Burke raised his hand over his head to congratulate him. "His hand was up in the air, and he was arching way back," recalled Baker. "So I reached up and hit his hand. It seemed like the thing to do." It was the world's first recorded high five.

Now the standard salute of celebrating athletes, the high five initially caught on as a symbol of gay pride. After retiring from baseball in 1980, Burke, the first openly gay professional baseball player, introduced the gesture of self-affirmation to residents of San Francisco's Castro district.

WAR IS OVER! (IF YOU PAY IT)
October 3, 2010

The Treaty of Versailles (1919) brought an end to the First World War, but its conditions weren't met for almost a century. On October 3, 2010, 92 years after Germany's defeat, the Central European nation finally paid off the last of its war reparations to the Allied Powers. World War I was, finally, officially over.

SHE'S LEAVING HOME
October 4, 1963

The seed for one of the most astonishing coincidences in music history was planted on this day when Paul McCartney appeared as a celebrity judge on a lip-syncing competition for the TV program *Ready, Steady, Go!* Four young girls danced and mimed for the adjudicating Beatle. He awarded first prize to contestant number 4, a 14-year-old girl named Melanie Coe. She came up to shake McCartney's hand and he gave her a signed Beatles album.

Four years later, Coe, now 17, quietly slipped out of her parents' house in the middle of the night, hopped a crosstown bus, and hightailed it to a friend's flat in Central London. McCartney read about the missing girl in the *Daily Mirror* and, not recognizing her name or her photograph, set her story to lyrics

In May 1967, "She's Leaving Home" appeared as the sixth track on the Beatles' *Sgt. Pepper's Lonely Hearts Club Band*. It would be years before McCartney connected the runaway from his song with the teenybopper he awarded first prize to in 1963.

THE MAN WHO WALKED AROUND THE WORLD
October 5, 1974

On this day, Dave Kunst staggered the final yards into his hometown of Waseca, Minnesota, to become the first person to circumnavigate the globe on foot—a four-year journey that took him through four continents, 13 countries, and 21 pairs of shoes.

Along the way he was shot in the chest by bandits in Afghanistan, partied with the Roma in Spain, and met Princess Grace of Monaco. He sloshed through Indian monsoons and trekked the hallowed Khyber Pass (reportedly the first non-Asian to do so since Alexander the Great). He also met his future wife.

In 2014, Kunst and his wife celebrated the 40th anniversary of his achievement by traveling from California to New York—by car. "The walking's over," he said.

DEATH OF THE HIPPIE
October 6, 1967

It's just as hard to pin down the birthdate of a mass movement as it is to pin down its death, but in the case of the hippies there appears to be a clear termination point. On October 6, 1967, on the one-year anniversary of LSD's illegalization and two short weeks after the end of the "Summer of Love," hippies in San Francisco's Haight-Ashbury held a funeral procession for "The Death of the Hippie"—intended simultaneously as a commemoration of the magical summer and a protest against the media's commercialization of the hippie movement.

After an early-morning wake at All Saint's Church, pallbearers carried a coffin filled with beads, hair, incense, and flowers through the streets. When they reached Buena Vista Park, on a hill overlooking Haight-Ashbury, they ceremonially burned the hippie artifacts.

UP
October 7, 1870

On this day, with France under siege by the Prussian army, Léon Gambetta, the French Minister of the Interior, escaped Paris in a hot-air balloon.

Couriers had been delivering letters and parcels to Paris by balloon for years, and as enemy forces closed in on the capital city, Gambetta knew it was his only chance to get out. On the morning of October 7, 1870, a large crowd assembled in Montmartre to see off their Interior Minister. Shouts of *"Vive la Republique! Vive Gambetta!"* followed the balloonist as he rose into the air, floating past the line of French forts and over enemy territory. As bullets whizzed past, the statesman calmly drifted onward, as though—in the words of one newspaper—"he were a log of wood floating down a river."

After Gambetta's highly public escape, ballooning sprang up in circuses across Europe. Some say it inspired the Wizard's flight from Oz in L. Frank Baum's 1900 novel.

THE KETTLE WAR
October 8, 1784

After years of tension between the Holy Roman Empire and the Dutch Republic, the two world powers battled in the waterways of Amsterdam on this day in 1784. After a single shot, the Empire surrendered.

Emperor Joseph II had sent out three warships, led by the vessel *Le Louis,* to take Amsterdam's Scheldt River. The Dutch dispatched one ship, the *Dolfijn,* to defend the Scheldt. When *Le Louis* came within range, the *Dolfijn* fired. The bullet ricocheted off the boat's armaments and spooked the captain into an immediate surrender.

The Kettle War got its name from its only casualty: a soup kettle on the deck of *Le Louis.*

THE MAN WHO TAUGHT ANDY WARHOL TO PAINT
October 9, 1984

On this day, a little-known 20-something tech prodigy with a Beatlesque hairdo attended a birthday party for Sean Lennon, the nine-year-old son of Yoko Ono and the late John Lennon. The guest list included many of New York's artistic elite—Keith Haring, John Cage, Louise Nevelson, Kenny Scharf, Andy Warhol. Standing among these giants, the young man was dwarfed nearly to obscurity.

After dinner, the nameless mingler gave Sean his birthday present—a "Macintosh" computer, fresh off its first production run. He set it up on the floor of Sean's bedroom and instructed him in the basics of MacPaint. Soon the other party guests gathered to admire the machine.

"Can I try?" Warhol asked. The techie obliged, and the 56-year-old artist got down on his hands and knees to take Sean's spot at the monitor. Warhol picked up the cigarette box-sized contraption (a "mouse," it was explained to him), but instead of gliding it on the floor he waved it over his head like a baton. The young man placed his hand on Warhol's and guided it as Warhol followed the motion of the paintbrush on the screen. "My God!" he exclaimed. "I drew a circle!"

Warhol later recalled the moment the whiz kid finally identified himself: "I said that once some man had been calling me a lot wanting to give me [a Macintosh], but that I'd never called him back or something, and then the kid looked up and said, 'Yeah, that was me. I'm Steve Jobs.'"

THE REAL WINNER
October 10, 1995

Dr. Robert Lucas, one of the most influential economists of the twentieth century, on this day won the 1995 Nobel Prize in Economics, but was allowed to keep only half of his one million dollar award. His ex-wife had a clause inserted in their 1989 divorce settlement guaranteeing her "50 percent of any Nobel Prize" he won before October 31, 1995. He beat the deadline by three weeks.

THE FIRST TOILET ON TV
October 11, 1957

For decades, television censors kept many ordinary aspects of life off the air: pregnant women, shared beds, belly buttons. Even the mere glimpse of a toilet was enough to send censors reeling.

In the pilot episode of *Leave It to Beaver,* Wally and Beaver order a baby alligator from an ad and hide it in their toilet tank, but this premise was deemed too dirty for 1950s television. The episode was bumped as the show's premiere and delayed for a week as producers figured out how to work around the lavatorial constraint. Ultimately, they decided to allow a single shot of the *back* of the tank, and the episode aired the following week.

And thus, on October 11, 1957, *Leave It to Beaver* became the first sitcom to show a toilet—and an alligator became the first TV character to use it.

THE MEN WHO STARE AT MANILA FOLDERS
October 12, 1988

In the last years of the Cold War, the United States invested millions of dollars training agents in psychic espionage. On October 12, 1988, during one of these training sessions, a military clairvoyant (known only as number 025) was asked to identify a photo of a famous individual inside of a closed manila envelope. The trainee closed his eyes, focused his second sight, and began describing traits as they came to him. His testimony has been recently declassified:

> *This individual is a man and he is deceased. He was old when he died. He was born in a foreign country. . . . He had charisma. People laughed at him. He's nostalgic.*
>
> *He looked like a hippie. He wore glasses and smoked a pipe. He made a fuss. He was a soul searcher. He had a sad nature.*
>
> *His life work concerned the sciences and people. He was extremely smart. He worked for the future and his work made a difference and he geared his work for the future. He was persistent in his work. He produced a lot of work. . . . Gorbochov [sic] is now involved with his work that involved substances. This man was also a teacher. . . .*
>
> *He had a life force personality. He was in* Life *and* Time *magazines and there are statues of him.*
>
> *Name of individual: Alfer Alfreman Alfermen Alfer*

It was Albert Einstein.

ONE FINE DAY
October 13, 1307

At dawn on Friday, October 13, 1307, Philip IV of France arrested and tortured scores of the Knights Templar on suspicion of heresy. According to Robert Langdon—a respected (fictional) Harvard University professor in Dan Brown's *Da Vinci Code* universe—this date is the origin for the unlucky "Friday the 13th" superstition.

The first specific reference to Friday the 13th as an unlucky day, however, wasn't made until the twentieth century, when Thomas W. Lawson picked it as the day of a Wall Street crash in his novel *Friday the Thirteenth (1907)*. Eerily, the schooner *Thomas W. Lawson,* named after the author, was caught in a storm and shipwrecked off the coast of England the same year his novel was published, just after midnight on Saturday, December 14, 1907. To Lawson, at home in Massachusetts, it was still Friday the 13th.

A REAL LAZYBONES
October 14, 1895

Albert Einstein was a lousy student. He distrusted authority, rebelled against his teachers, and at 15 dropped out of high school. Hoping to skip his last year of required schooling and jump straight into university, he applied to the Polytechnic Institute in Zürich but flunked his entrance exam on October 14, 1895. (He aced the math part, but failed the language and history sections.) When he finally did get in the following year, he cut most of his classes and copied notes from a classmate.

One professor at Polytechnic wrote Einstein a sanction in the school record: "March 1899: reprimand from the Director on account of lack of diligence in the Physics Practicum." Another professor called his delinquent student "a real lazybones" who "never bothered about mathematics at all."

THAT DARN CAT
October 15, 1910

On this day, Walter Wellman launched the airship *America* from Atlantic City in the world's first attempt to fly across the Atlantic Ocean. He brought along a five-person crew, a spark gap radio set, and a cat named Kiddo for good luck.

Kiddo didn't like being airborne. "I am chiefly worried by our cat," wrote navigator F. Murray Simon in his log, fifteen minutes after takeoff. "[He] is rushing around the airship like a squirrel in a cage."

Jack Irwin, the wireless radio operator, who was stationed in a lifeboat suspended below the airship, heard the commotion overhead. "This cat is raising hell!" he cried out. "I believe it's going mad!" and he insisted they pass it down to a motorboat before getting too far out to sea. Simon refused: "We must keep the cat at all costs; we can never have luck without a cat aboard."

Melvin Vaniman, the chief engineer, was so annoyed by the turbulent cargo that he radioed back to land for assistance. Thus, the world's first air-to-ground radio transmission was this:

"Roy, come and get this goddamn cat!"

TEAM OF KINGS
October 16, 1384

On this day, a 10-year-old Hungarian girl named Hedwig was crowned King of Poland.

When her father Louis the Great, who reigned as king of Hungary and Poland, died in 1382, his domain was split between his two daughters—Mary taking Hungary and Hedwig taking Poland. But while the elder Mary became Hungary's queen regnant (a female monarch equivalent in rank to a king), the Polish order decided that Hedwig, given her age, would be treated with more respect holding a masculine royal title. In a ceremony in Krakow in 1384, the Hungarian preteen officially became Poland's new king.

When he learned of her kinghood, William of Habsburg, Hedwig's prearranged suitor, hurried to Krakow to claim Hedwig's hand. Hedwig turned him down and instead married Jogaila, the Grand Duke of Lithuania, who then assumed the same title as Hedwig. For 15 years, Hedwig and Jogaila ruled Poland as a husband-and-wife team of kings.

THE LONDON BEER FLOOD
October 17, 1814

On this day, in the London parish of St. Giles, a huge wooden vat holding a million pints of beer burst open, unleashing an amber wave of porter rushing into Bainbridge Street. The 15-foot-high cascade plowed through two homes, crushed the Tavistock Arms Pub, and claimed the lives of eight people.

A jury acquitted the brewers of wrongdoing, judging the incident to be an "Act of God." Although no plaque or memorial exists on the site today, a nearby pub—The Holborn Whippet—brews a special anniversary porter each year on October 17 to commemorate the London Beer Flood.

THE NORFOLK OEDIPUS
October 18, 1730

In 1702, a widow named Alice Johnson married her farmhand, a young man named Christopher Burraway, at Norwich Cathedral in Norfolk, England. Christopher's father had been married to Mary Lane, who, when he died, remarried to Gregory Johnson— who had just come out of a marriage with Alice Johnson. By marrying his father's widow's husband's ex-wife, Christopher was in quite the familial entanglement. Let's let his tombstone explain:

> *Here lyeth the body of*
> *Christopher Burraway who*
> *Departed this life ye 18th day*
> *of October Anno Domini 1730*
> *Aged 59 years.*
> *And Thir lyes Alice*
> *Who By hir Life*
> *Was my sister, my mistress,*
> *My mother and my wife.*

STARVING ARTIST
October 19, 2003

David Blaine certainly has his critics, but nothing drew a frenzy of trollish haters quite like his stunt over London in 2003. That September, the endurance artist locked himself inside a clear plastic box 30 feet over the south bank of the River Thames. For 44 days, Blaine survived only on water. More than a quarter of a million Londoners came out to see the artist waste away in his cage—many just to taunt him. The so-called "Blaine-baiters" hurled raw eggs, tomatoes, and paint-filled balloons. One blew an air horn whenever Blaine tried to sleep. Another beat a drum. A hamburger was flown up to his enclosure with a remote-controlled helicopter. Women flashed their breasts, and men their buttocks. One man practiced his tee shot from 60 yards off using Blaine as a target.

When Blaine emerged from suspension on October 19, he had lost 25 percent of his body weight and was suffering from heart palpitations and blurred vision. But he had nothing but love for his taunters. "I've learned how important it is to have a sense of humor and laugh at everything, because nothing makes sense anymore. I love all of you forever." He was promptly hospitalized.

TAKE YOUR PICK
October 20, 1897

A long, drawn-out custody battle came to an unusual—but surprisingly convenient—resolution on this day in the small city of Butte, Montana. *The Butte Daily Post* reported:

> When the matter came up in court, Judge Clancy asked the boys which they liked best, their father or mother; the younger, aged 8 years, answered "mother" and the older, 9 years, said "father." That settled it. The mother got the former and the father the latter.

LITEROTICA
October 21, 1556

Dirty stories are probably as old as language itself, but the first modern literary pornographer (according to scholars of smut) was the Renaissance poet Pietro Aretino. His first erotic work, the *Lust Sonnets,* are a series of ribald poems making sexual innuendo out of battlefield imagery—broadsword, lancet, arrows, and others of that phallic ilk. They caused such outrage in Rome that the poet fled for his life to Venice, where he wrote his most famous work, *Ragionamenti,* in which Aretino originated the "whore dialogue"—an erotic genre of the Renaissance wherein an older, more experienced prostitute explains sex to a younger one through use of pornographic tales.

He died the way he lived—with smut on his mind. On October 21, 1556, Aretino was listening to his sister tell a dirty joke when he plunged into a fit of laughter, keeled back, and croaked. Depending on the account, Aretino either died falling off his chair or by asphyxiation from the giggling itself.

HAPPY EARTHDAY
October 22, 4004 B.C.

According to seventeenth century Archbishop James Ussher, the earth was created at precisely 6 p.m. on October 22, 4004 B.C.—a Saturday. He arrived at that date based on his interpretation of the rise and fall of the great empires, the reigns of the biblical kings, Adamic genealogy, Johannes Kepler's astronomical tables, and the birth of Jesus Christ. Once he figured the year of Creation, Ussher counted back from the autumnal equinox (the Jewish year begins in autumn) to the next closest Sunday, and from there rewound another six hours from midnight to get his date. That makes Adam a Scorpio.

THE ICEMAN CURSETH
October 23, 2004

Helmut Simon had been hiking with his wife Erika in Austria's Ötztal range in September 1991 when they spotted the preserved body of a prehistoric man jutting out of the ice. The discovery became an archaeological sensation, in part for its tantalizing clues about Ötzi the Iceman's final days and speculated murder. (An arrowhead was lodged in his shoulder and blood from at least four other people was found on his gear.) In 2004, while hiking near that same Alpine spot, Simon went missing. A rescue team scoured the area for eight days. His body was finally discovered on October 23, frozen in a stream below Gaiskarkogel Peak. Unlike his Copper Age counterpart, Simon's corpse showed no signs of foul play. It's believed Simon died quickly and painlessly, slipping off a precipice 300 feet above.

DEATHBED RAVINGS
October 24, 1935

New York mobster Dutch Schultz survived for 29 hours after being shot at the urinal of a restaurant bathroom. In the hospital, a police stenographer took down his last babbling words. Some highlights from the transcript:

> *"It is no use to stage a riot. The sidewalk was in trouble and the bears were in trouble, and I broke it up."*

> *"There are only ten of us. There are ten million fighting somewhere of you, so get your onions up and we will throw up the truce flag."*

> *"Oh, oh, dog biscuits and when he is happy he doesn't get snappy."*

> *"I am a pretty good pretzler. Winifred. Department of Justice. I even get it from the department."*

> *"You can play jacks, and girls do that with a soft ball and do tricks with it."*

> *"A boy has never wept nor dashed a thousand kim. Did you hear me?"*

> *"Communistic—strike—baloney—honestly this is a habit I get."*

> *"Please put me in that room. Please keep him in control. My gilt-edged stuff and those dirty rats have tuned in."*

> *"I am half crazy. They won't let me get up. They dyed my shoes."*

> *"Please help me up, Henry. Max, come over here. French-Canadian bean soup."*

Inspired by these deathbed ravings, the Beat writer William Burroughs wrote a 1970 screenplay, *The Last Words of Dutch Schultz*, shaped around the mobster's nonsensical statements. Authors Robert Shea and Robert Anton Wilson, meanwhile, linked Schultz's last words to an Illuminati conspiracy in their 1975 *The Illuminatus! Trilogy*.

DEAD BALL
October 25, 1998

During a soccer match in the Congolese village of Bena Tshadi, a lightning bolt killed all 11 members of the home team. Miraculously, the visiting team emerged completely unhurt.

The survivors were accused of hiring witchdoctors to hex their opponents (an alleged practice among athletes in voodoo-steeped Central Africa) and were intimidated out of town by locals. Investigators later discovered that the players on the home team wore metal screw-in spikes, while the visitors wore plastic.

CRIMSON DAWN
October 26, 1929

On this day, red became the official color of all London buses, beating out green and yellow in a pigment war that dated back to the 1800s.

Between 1859 and 1929, London's transport system fell under the operation of several private companies, and vehicles came in different shades depending on the route owner. In 1907, the London General Omnibus Company, painted its entire fleet bright red to stand out. As the LGOC grew, Londoners expected a certain hue from their double-decker liveries. When London consolidated its private bus companies in 1929 under the government-owned "London Transport," it rouged all its buses to look the same.

The precise shade of red paint used on London buses is Pantone 485 C, the same used on the London Underground, Kit Kat bars, and McDonald's restaurants.

FORBIDDEN FRUIT
October 27, 1439

On this day, King Albert II of Germany dropped dead from eating too many melons. The 42-year-old monarch was enjoying his afternoon feast when he came down with a bout of indigestion and collapsed.

He's not the only historical figure to perish from eating this sweet fruit to excess. Pope Paul II, Pope Clement VII, Maximilian I Archduke of Austria, and Frederick the Great are all said to have died by melon overdose. King John of England died in 1216 from a surfeit of peaches.

WELL-HEELED
October 28, 1533

At her wedding to the Duke of Orleans in Marseille, Catherine de Medici wore the first pair of high heels in recorded history. They were constructed for the petite 14-year-old bride so she could stand confidently alongside the towering Diane de Poitiers, the Duke's long-legged mistress, over whom Catherine had her obvious insecurities.

Other French aristocrats soon adopted the skyscraping footwear (including, most famously, King Louis XIV, who would wear four-inch platforms decorated with battle scenes), and heels naturally became associated with class. People of authority started being referred to as "well-heeled," while those of lower standing were "down at the heels."

PATIENCE IS A VIRTUE
October 29, 1880

Pulling into port off the coast of Norfolk, the *Ocean Queen* was caught in a storm and run aground. The local townspeople sent a small sailboat to the aid of the distressed ship, but the life-saving vessel hit a large wave and capsized. Its mast stuck in the sand and its anchor dropped out, pinning it upside-down and killing 11 of its 13 men. At low tide, the crew of the *Ocean Queen* simply walked ashore.

MARS ATTACKS
October 30, 1938

On this night, radio listeners tuning in to their regular Sunday-evening programming heard instead a terrifying news bulletin: Martians were invading New Jersey. Frightened families huddled around their console radios, listening nervously as reporters in the field described black, serpent-like creatures—"large as a bear," glistening "like wet leather"—emerging from metal spacecraft, equipped with heat-ray guns that could take out an entire army in a flash of green light and smoke.

The news report, of course, was not real. It was a radio adaptation of the H. G. Wells novel *The War of the Worlds* for a special Halloween episode of the CBS drama series *Mercury Theatre on the Air*. The man behind it, a baby-faced, 23-year-old wunderkind by the name of Orson Welles—soon to be known for his cinematic masterpiece *Citizen Kane*—had no idea how much panic his little production would cause.

After the Martians wipe out the vanguard of crash site reporters, they sprout legs from their metal pods and grow to the size of trees. Some listeners, driven to hallucination in their heightened excitement, actually "saw" these tentacled colossi high-stepping through the New Jersey Palisades. Others described seeing veils of green smoke outside their windows, hanging ominously over the Manhattan skyline. In the town of Princeton Junction, terrified locals shot up their neighborhood water tower, believing it to be an alien spaceship. A resident of Grover's Mill, ground zero of the phony Martian strike, called the police department, screaming, "You can't imagine the horror of it! It's hell!"

According to later surveys, of the 12 million who tuned in to Welles's broadcast, about one million listeners truly believed that Martian killing machines on tripod legs had descended upon

Earth and were annihilating its population with heat-ray guns. Emergency switchboards lit up through the night with questions about evacuation procedures and gas-raid shelters, and at least one report came in of someone tumbling down the stairs lugging heavy suitcases, overstuffed for the apocalypse.

THE GREAT SCHNOZZOLA
October 31, 1945

Jimmy Durante's prominent nose was his trademark. He referred to it as his "Schnozzle" or "Schnozzola," and made so many jokes about it that he became known as "The Schnoz." (In the 1930s, he insured his nose with Lloyd's of London for $140,000.) When invited to leave his handprints in the cement outside Grauman's Chinese Theatre, he imprinted his bulbous beak instead. Underneath he wrote, "Dis is my Schnozzle. Wish I had a Million of 'Em. Jimmy Durante. Oct-31-45."

THE SHOW WINDOW
November 1, 1897

In 1900, L. Frank Baum published two books. One was about a Kansas girl who gets sucked into a tornado and winds up in a wonderful land called Oz. The other was a manual on how to decorate dry goods windows.

Baum developed his passion for "window trimming"—the art of arranging attractive displays in shop windows—while running his retail store Baum's Bazaar in South Dakota. On November 1, 1897, three years shy of his commercial breakthrough, Baum published his first literary work—the inaugural issue of *The Show Window*, the first ever magazine devoted to window trimming. Four months later he founded the National Association of Window Trimmers.

THE GREAT EMU WAR
November 2, 1932

After the First World War ended, Australia rewarded its veterans with farmland in the untamed western part of the continent. But the returning soldiers soon faced an army of a different sort when a horde of emus stormed in, ravaging the land, spoiling the harvest, and tearing down fencing that left the farms vulnerable to other pests. Australian Minister of Defense Sir George Pearce saw only one option: war.

On November 2, 1932, Pearce deployed troops to the wild outback armed with Lewis machine guns, 10,000 rounds of ammunition, and military trucks, and charged them to bring back "100 emu skins." But the six-foot flightless bird proved a tough adversary. When soldiers tried to ambush a herd of 50 emus near the town of Campion, the birds scattered every which way, avoiding most of the bullets and seeming to repel the rest off their thick hides. "They can face machine-guns with the invulnerability of tanks," said one soldier. "There's only one way to kill an emu," said another. "Shoot him through the back of the head when his mouth is closed or through the front of his mouth when his mouth is open. That's how hard it is."

As the war progressed, the emus appeared to take up standard military tactics. "Each pack seems to have its leader now," reported an army correspondent, "a big black-plumed bird which stands fully six feet high and keeps watch while his mates carry out their work of destruction and warns them of our approach."

Major G.P.W. Meredith, the commander of the eradicating army, admitted he'd grossly underestimated his enemy: "If we had a military division with the bullet-carrying capacity of these birds," he said, "it would face any army in the world."

After six days, the soldiers had spent a quarter of their ammunition killing less than 50 birds. When the press reported on the fruitless operation, Pearce decided to save his troops from further humiliation and ordered them back home. The emus had won.

THE BATTLE OF THE BEES
November 3, 1914

On this morning, the British Indian Army was trying to sneak up on Tanga, a key African seaport held by the Germans, when they upset dozens of beehives hovering in hollow logs above the battlefield. The bees emerged in clouds, chaos ensued, and the British rushed back to their ships like "jibbering idiots" and leapt into the sea to avoid the painful stings.

"I would never have believed that grown-up men of any race could have been reduced to such shamelessness," remarked one British officer.

The British called a truce the next day.

WHEN PIGS FLY
November 4, 1909

On this day, English aviation pioneer John Moore-Brabazon (later the Minister of Transport under Winston Churchill during World War II) achieved the first "live cargo" plane flight: he put a pig in a wicker basket, tied it to a wing strut of his French *Voisin* airplane, and took off.

He named the animal Icarus II, after the airman of Greek mythology, and attached a sign on the basket certifying the famously impossible event. It read: "I AM THE FIRST PIG TO FLY."

THE SCATOLOGICAL COMPOSER (OR, THE SECOND MOVEMENT)
November 5, 1777

"Oui, by the love of my skin, I s*** on your nose, so it runs down your chin."

—Wolfgang Amadeus Mozart, in a letter to his young cousin, Maria Anna

Mozart wrote roughly 39 of these so-called "scatological letters"—epistles to his family and friends on the subject of excrement. In 1798, Mozart's wife Constanze sent a batch of them to the publisher Breitkopf & Härtel for use in a biography. In her accompanying letter, she disclaimed, "Although in dubious taste, the letters . . . are full of wit and deserve mentioning, although they cannot of course be published in their entirety."

The couplet above, from a letter dated November 5, 1777 (translated by Robert Spaethling), was probably an inside joke between Mozart and his 19-year-old cousin, with whom the poop-obsessed composer kept up a regular scatological correspondence. He winds up the letter in similar poetic fashion:

"I now wish you a good night, s*** in your bed with all your might, sleep with peace on your mind, and try to kiss your own behind."

GRAND THEFT PARSONS
November 6, 1973

American record producer and tour manager Phil Kaufman was notorious for his wild road exploits—the most famous of which involved stealing the body of Gram Parsons and setting it on fire in the California desert.

Shortly before the country singer died in September 1973, he and Kaufman swore a mutual pact: whichever of the two died first, the other would have his remains cremated at the base of Cap Rock in Joshua Tree National Park. But when Parsons passed away, his estranged father demanded the body be flown back to the family home in Louisiana (where, it was said, he wanted his son buried so he could make a claim to the singer's massive estate). Kaufman and his assistant Michael Martin rented a funeral hearse, dressed up as mortuary workers, and signed out Parsons's body from Los Angeles International Airport before it could be shipped to New Orleans. Out at Joshua Tree, Kaufman poured gas into the casket and torched it under the desert sky.

Campers reported the harsh smoke to authorities, and the body-snatching duo was quickly arrested. The court case didn't last long. On November 6, 1973, the day after what would have been Parsons's 27th birthday, Kaufman and Martin were found guilty—but only of destroying the casket. In a strange holdover from English common law, California had no legal statute at the time against stealing a body. A grave robber could be charged with desecration of a grave, destruction of property, or theft of a corpse's personal belongings (jewelry, clothes, and the like)—but not with theft of the body itself. Kaufman and Martin paid $300 apiece for the casket and walked free.

THE CURSE OF TIPPECANOE
November 7, 1811

On this date, William Henry Harrison's army prevailed over the Shawnee leader Tecumseh in the Battle of Tippecanoe, supposedly inciting a curse wherein every U.S. president elected at 20-year intervals died in office, beginning with Harrison.

Harrison (elected in 1840) caught a cold and croaked after a month as president; Abraham Lincoln (elected in 1860), James Garfield (1880), and William McKinley (1900) all died by assassination; Warren G. Harding (1920) and Franklin Delano Roosevelt (1940) died natural deaths in office; John F. Kennedy (1960), also, by assassination.

Ronald Reagan, elected in 1980, finally broke the "Curse of Tippecanoe" when he survived a gunshot to the chest—though credit may be due to his wife, Nancy. The notoriously superstitious First Lady hired astrologers to shield her husband from the curse.

TWO OF US
November 8, 2005

On this day, 23-year-old Candace Dickinson was ticketed on the Phoenix interstate for driving alone in the carpool lane—a lane reserved for vehicles with two or more passengers. When the officer asked if she had anyone else in the car, Candace Dickinson replied "yes" and pointed to her belly.

In court, Dickinson claimed that her pregnancy should legally count as a second passenger. "Whether my son is in a car seat versus in my stomach, I don't get it," she said. "It's the same thing." Judge Dennis Freeman disagreed, explaining that the carpool lane law requires a passenger to occupy a "separate and distinct . . . empty space in a vehicle." Furthermore, should he uphold Dickinson's claim, police would have to begin carrying around pregnancy testers—"and I don't think we want to go there." He fined Dickinson $367.

The temptation to cheat the carpool lane is apparently strong. Six days before Dickinson's ticketing, a man was pulled over in California for driving in a carpool lane with a legless kickboxing dummy, dressed in a hat and coat, strapped into the passenger seat.

THIS IS THE END
November 9, 2013

The once-dominant chain Blockbuster closed its doors for good in early 2014, marking the end of the video rental era. As fate would have it, the last Blockbuster title ever rented was the Seth Rogen comedy *This Is the End*. It was checked out at 11 p.m. on November 9, 2013, at a store in Hawaii.

THE KIDNAPPING OF DAN RATHER
November 10, 1980

During a routine cab ride to a Chicago address, CBS anchorman Dan Rather's driver got lost and drove around in circles for half an hour searching for the house. When they finally arrived, Rather, temper flaring, tried to stiff the cabbie over the fare. The driver instead locked the doors and drove off with the newscaster still inside.

An off-duty policewoman on her way to work noticed "a man gesticulating rather madly in the backseat of a taxi cab," and a high-speed chase ensued. She pursued the cab down quiet lakeside streets, through busy city blocks and thoroughfares, until finally pinning it at a red light. The driver was arrested for kidnapping a passenger. CBS ended up footing the $12.55 fare.

CORDUROY APPRECIATION DAY
November 11, 2011

The annual gathering of the Corduroy Appreciation Club takes place on the eleventh of November—11/11—the date that, in the view of its founder, Miles Rohan, most resembles the vertical lines of corduroy.

On 11/11/11, the club held its "Grandest Meeting" in New York City, featuring a corduroy fashion show, history lecture, poetry reading, and a keynote delivered by comedian and "corduphile" Amy Sedaris. The event drew thousands of cord fashionistas (film director Wes Anderson missed the event, but sent his regrets in a personal letter), and at the end of the night crowned a Corduroy Messiah, a young girl who turned 11 on 11/11/11.

BE FAIR TO LONG HAIR
November 12, 1964

Before David Bowie was Ziggy Stardust or Major Tom—before he was even David Bowie—he was David Jones, the seventeen-year-old president of a very bizarre British society. On November 12, 1964, the future rock star sat for an interview with the BBC to discuss his newly formed organization, The Society for the Prevention of Cruelty to Long-Haired Men.

"I think we're all fairly tolerant," explained Bowie, "but for the last two years we've had comments like 'Darling!' and 'Can I carry your handbag?' thrown at us, and I think it just has to stop now."

The program's host, Cliff Michelmore, asked if such comments surprised the mop-topped teenager—since, "after all, you've got really rather long hair, haven't you?"

"We have, yes," Bowie replied, flanked by eleven inches of golden locks. "I think we all like long hair, and we don't see why other people should persecute us because of this."

Five months after his television appearance, the BBC dared ask the singer to cut his hair before a live performance with his band the Manish Boys. In response, Bowie organized a picket outside the BBC with placards bearing his society's slogan—"Be fair to long hair!"

THE GREEN FEATHER MOVEMENT
November 13, 1953

On this day, in the midst of America's "Red Scare," the Indiana Textbook Commission declared the character Robin Hood a Communist and ordered all references to the bow-slinger—who famously stole from the rich to give to the poor—stricken from state schoolbooks.

To protest the censorship, five students from Indiana University collected several burlap sacksful of chicken feathers from a local farm, dyed them green to represent the feather worn by Robin Hood, and distributed them around campus in commencement of what they termed the Green Feather Movement.

The controversy reached all the way to the actual Sheriff of Nottingham, whose predecessor of some 900 years had, according to legend, chased Robin and his Merry Men round about Sherwood Forest. "We're very proud of Robin Hood," said the lawman of his city's famous outlaw. "Although if he were alive today . . . I'd have to do my duty and go out after him."

The Indiana State Superintendent of Education also came to Robin's defense. "[The story] sounds all right as I remember," he said, "but it's been twenty-five years since I read it." After rereading *The Merry Adventures of Robin Hood*—just to make sure—he overturned the ban.

FINNISH BASEBALL
November 14, 1920

One of the stranger sports played on this planet is *pesäpallo*, or Finnish baseball. Born in a park in Helsinki on November 14, 1920, *pesäpallo* is the brainchild of Finnish track and field athlete Lauri Pihkala, who is said to have visited America in 1907, watched one baseball game, and decided it was too boring. In Pihkala's livelier version, players run in a zigzag base pattern rather than counterclockwise; triples count as home runs; and instead of sitting in the dugouts, the offensive team stands in a semicircle around the pitcher and heckles him. A scout for the Minnesota Twins once said, "If you dropped acid and decided to go make baseball, this is what you would end up with."

THE SPOON LADY
November 15, 1959

On this day, for the second time in three years, The Beatles—known then as The Quarrymen—lost in the preliminary round of Carroll Levis's *TV Star Search* competition. (The winner got to play on live television.) The first time, they lost to a dwarf playing tea-chest bass. This time, it was to a woman playing the spoons.

The spoon lady was a bane of The Beatles' early existence. "She always creamed us, this old lady," recalled Paul McCartney. "I think she used to follow us round, the bastard. 'Where are the Beatles trying this week? I'll beat 'em. I've got the measure of them.'"

BANKER SPANKER
November 16, 1979

In 1978, a Pittsburgh-area bank manager named David Rhodes was caught spanking customers who were tardy with their loan payments.

His victims ultimately blackmailed him for $88,268 by threatening to report his behavior to authorities. When auditors caught Rhodes stealing funds to cover his tracks, the 38-year-old banker admitted that he'd been paddling the buttocks of delinquent customers in his office for years.

On November 16, 1979, Rhodes was sentenced to three years in a Pennsylvania prison for misappropriating bank funds. One newspaper ran the all-time great headline, "Ex-Banker, Spanker, Winds up in Tanker."

THE *HEIDI* BOWL
November 17, 1968

One of the all-time great football comebacks was missed by millions of viewers because of a TV scheduling conflict. On November 17, 1968, with 61 seconds remaining and the New York Jets up 3 against their rival the Oakland Raiders, NBC made the controversial decision to cut away to the TV movie *Heidi*. Suddenly, viewers were high up in the Swiss Alps watching a young girl prance around in a green skirt and sun hat, while down in Oakland the Raiders were staging a legendary rally, scoring two touchdowns in the final minute to win 43 to 32.

The *Heidi* Bowl, as it became known, roused fans to a white-hot fury. NBC groveled for forgiveness the next day.

TALK TURKEY
November 18, 1889

From this day's edition of the *Brooklyn Daily Eagle*:

> *John Snyder, a big, burly peddler, who on Saturday night bit the head off a turkey in a saloon at 38 Varet Street, was arraigned before Justice Kenna this morning on a charge of cruelty to animals. The details were published in yesterday's Eagle. Snyder pleaded guilty.*
>
> *"It was on a wager," exclaimed the prisoner. "The owner of the turkey was satisfied."*
>
> *"But I suppose the turkey had no say in the matter," remarked Justice Kenna.*

Snyder was sent to jail for twenty-nine days.

ONE HELLUVA FILM
November 19, 1925

In 2013, *The Wolf of Wall Street* set a new record as the most profane Hollywood film ever made, with 569 utterances of the F-word alone. (That's 3.16 per minute.) After a profanity pummeling like that, it's hard to believe there was a time when a single *damn* sent movie critics into a tizzy. The first Hollywood movie to include profanity was *The Big Parade:* It opened on November 19, 1925, at New York's Astor Theater, and featured a whopping three curse words over the span of 2 hours and 21 minutes. As it was a silent film, the words *goddamn, helluva,* and *bitches* all appeared on title cards.

SUBSTITUTE
November 20, 1973

When Keith Moon collapsed onstage from an overdose of animal tranquilizers, Pete Townshend invited a 19-year-old fan from the front row to fill in on drums for the rest of the show.

Scot Halpin had arrived at the Cow Palace in San Francisco thirteen hours early to get good seats for The Who concert. About seventy minutes in, Moon's drum kit went silent: the drummer was slumped over his snare, unconscious.

"Can anybody play the drums?" Townshend asked the crowd. "I mean somebody good!" Halpin's friend started shouting, "He can play! He can play!" In fact, Halpin hadn't played in over a year; nevertheless, when the concert promoter came over and asked, "Can you do it?" the teenager replied, straight out, "Yes."

Halpin was led onstage to Moon's drum kit and given a shot of brandy. "I'm going to lead you," Townshend said. "I'm going to cue you."

The band launched into "Smokestack Lightning," a straight blues jam, and Halpin filled in well enough. He continued through another blues number, stumbled through the more complex "Naked Eye," and the show ended. The teenager joined Townshend, Roger Daltrey, and John Entwistle center stage for a bow.

After the show, Halpin was brought backstage and given a leather Who jacket, which somebody stole later that evening.

JAILHOUSE ROCK
November 21

November 21 is a day of criminal peril for music-makers:

1980: Don Henley of the Eagles was arrested for possession of marijuana, cocaine, and Quaaludes, and for contributing to the delinquency of a minor.

1995: Green Day's Billie Joe Armstrong was arrested for mooning his audience at a concert in Milwaukee and fined $141.

1997: American rapper Coolio was charged with theft and assault at a boutique in the town of Böblingen, Germany.

2001: Jonathan King, the record producer who discovered the band Genesis, was sentenced to seven years in prison for multiple counts of child molestation.

2003: Michael Jackson was arrested in Santa Barbara, California, on multiple charges of child molestation.

2003: Record producer Phil Spector was charged with the murder of Lana Clarkson at his home the previous February.

WHODUNNIT?
November 22, 1987

At 11:15 p.m. on this day, a Chicago-area broadcast of *Doctor Who* abruptly cut to a video feed of a masked man in a suit and sunglasses getting spanked by a flyswatter. The signal hijack lasted about 90 seconds—during which time the man hummed the theme song to the 1950s animated show *Clutch Cargo,* crushed a Pepsi can, and gave the camera the finger. To this day, the hackers have never been identified.

THERE'S NO TOMORROW
November 23, 1958

Celebrity roasts rely heavily on shock value, but even today's raunchiest comics couldn't shock an audience as much as Harry Einstein did at the New York Friars Club roast of Lucille Ball and Desi Arnaz.

On November 23, 1958, Einstein, a middling radio comic (and father of comedic actor Albert Brooks), performed a brilliant nine-minute set that knocked the crowd dead, in show business parlance. When he returned to his seat on the dais, emcee Art Linkletter asked into the microphone, "Why isn't he on the air in primetime?" Einstein hardly registered the compliment before a pain stabbed his chest and he lurched into the lap of Milton Berle beside him. The crowd erupted in laughter, thinking it was an ad-lib, but the crisis was real. Einstein was having a heart attack.

The comic was rushed backstage, where a doctor from the audience sliced open his chest with a pocket scalpel to massage his heart. Meanwhile, out on the stage, Berle—in the spirit of *the show must go on*—urged Tony Martin to stall the crowd with an upbeat tune. Without thinking, the balladeer began belting out his big closer, "There's No Tomorrow." Berle tugged at his pant leg to stop but Martin went on, obliviously crooning out those morbidly ill-timed lyrics—"There's no tomorrow, there's just tonight"—as Einstein breathed his last breath backstage.

A NEW DISH
November 24, 1762

Edward Gibbon, the author of the landmark six-volume tome *The History of the Decline and Fall of the Roman Empire,* was quite fond of sandwiches—a newfangled food invented by his friend, the Earl of Sandwich. In a journal entry dated November 24, 1762, Gibbon made the world's first written mention of the sandwich:

> *I dined at the Cocoa Tree. . . . Twenty or thirty, perhaps, of the first men in the kingdom, in point of fashion and fortune, supping at little tables covered with a napkin, in the middle of a coffee-room, upon a bit of cold meat, or a Sandwich.*

As for the eponymous Earl, he invented the snack to sustain long sprees at the gambling table. In 1765, Pierre-Jean Grosley described the Earl of Sandwich at work:

> *A minister of state passed four and twenty hours at a public gaming-table, so absorpt in play, that, during the whole time, he had no subsistence but a piece of beef, between two slices of toasted bread, which he eat [sic] without ever quitting the game. This new dish grew highly in vogue, during my residence in London; it was called by the name of the minister who invented it.*

The bread kept the Earl's fingers greaseless, allowing him to fan out his cards with one hand and feed himself with the other. His fellow gamblers took notice and began to order "the same as Sandwich." And thus was born a new dish.

THE ART OF SEPPUKU
November 25, 1970

Yukio Mishima's 1961 short story "Patriotism" is remembered for its vivid description of *seppuku,* the ancient Samurai honor suicide of self-disembowelment. Mishima had a lifelong fascination with *seppuku:* as a child he fantasized of dying this valorous hero's death, and when he adapted "Patriotism" to the big screen in 1966 he cast himself as the disgraced soldier who carries out the bloody ritual.

Not until 1970, however, did Mishima perform the ritual for real. On November 25, 1970, the three-time Nobel Prize nominee led a coup d'état against the Japanese government. With the help of four Tatenokai militiamen, Mishima raided Japan's military headquarters, took a hostage, and seized control of the commanding general's office. Hoping to exhort more rebels to follow him, Mishima read a prepared manifesto from the office balcony to the soldiers gathered below. Instead of followers, he got jeers. As police helicopters swirled overhead, Mishima accepted his failure. He had only one thing left to do. He retreated into the office, knelt down on a mat, and drove a Samurai sword into his stomach.

The ritual was not yet complete. As Mishima writhed in agony, his assistant drew his own sword and—per *seppuku* tradition—mercifully beheaded his commander.

POP CRITIC
November 26, 1862

In a letter to a friend dated November 26, 1862, English novelist George Eliot coined the term "pop" music while complaining about a recent concert. "There is too much 'Pop' for the thorough enjoyment of the chamber music," Eliot wrote. (At that time, *pop* likely meant bouncy or lively rather than an abbreviation for *popular,* as it's used today.)

THE BERNERS STREET HOAX
November 27, 1810

Theodore Hook, the British inventor of the postcard, didn't always use the Royal Mail for good. A consummate practical joker, Hook once bet a friend that he could make any ordinary house the most talked-about house in all of London—a wager he won by mailing out nearly a thousand letters in the name of Mrs. Tottenham, a West End widow, requesting various deliveries and services to her home on an appointed day. The prank began before dawn on November 27, 1810, when a chimney sweep knocked at 54 Berners Street. No sooner did Mrs. Tottenham turn him away than another sweep appeared, followed by another and another—a dozen in all. Deliverymen soon arrived bearing wedding cakes, pianos, and furniture, and as the half-asleep widow grappled to keep them all at bay they were joined by a throng of fishmongers, shoemakers, undertakers, midwives, wig-makers, carpet-makers, doctors, lawyers, vicars, and priests, all summoned by Hook's mischievous missives. Word spread of a grand fete and crowds flocked to Berners Street in time to catch the Duke of York pull up in his carriage, bidden to the residence to supposedly take the deathbed confession of a local councilman.

By the afternoon, the few merry lanes leading to Mrs. Tottenham's door were choked with carriage traffic, which backed up into the thoroughfares, causing chaos and gridlock in London's West End. *The Morning Post* described the scene the next day:

> *The greatest hoax that ever has been heard of in this metropolis was yesterday practised in Berners street, Oxford street. The house of Mrs. Tottenham, a Lady of fortune, at No. 54, was beset by about a dozen tradespeople at one time, with*

their various commodities, and from the confusion altogether
such crowds had collected as to render the street impassable.
Waggons laden with coals from the Paddington wharfs,
upholsterer's goods in cart loads, organs, piano fortes, linens,
jewellery, and every other description of furniture sufficient
to have stocked the whole street, were lodged as near as
possible to the door of 54, with anxious tradespeople and a
laughing mob.

Hook, who had been watching the drama develop from a distance, slipped away when the police showed up. He feigned an illness and lay up in bed for a week, after which he "recuperated" with a country tour. By the time he returned to London the storm had blown over, and Hook's hoax was but a distant, chaotic memory—more traumatic for some than others.

PLAY ON WORDS
November 28, 1582

The spelling of William Shakespeare's name is a matter of scholarly debate. Of the six signatures he left behind, no two are spelled alike, and Will's surname appears on official documents variously as Sakspere, Shakespeer, Shaxpyere, and Shaxpeare. He saved his wittiest moniker for his wedding day. On November 28, 1582, the notorious punster signed his marriage license "William Shagspeare"—perhaps a bawdy joke in anticipation of the consummation.

WRITER'S BLOCK
November 29, 1967

Truman Capote, Ernest Hemingway, and Virginia Woolf all suffered creative dry spells, but Ralph Ellison's 41-year stalemate with his sophomore novel, *Juneteenth,* is generally considered literature's most severe case of writer's block. (Some say it was the novel that killed him.) His blockage grew considerably worse after a tragic setback in the fall of 1967. On November 29, after laboring for 15 years over *Juneteenth,* a fire burned down his New England summerhouse, taking portions of his manuscript along with it. The tragedy reportedly broke Ellison's spirit and he never published *Juneteenth*—or any another novel—again.

ONE AND A MILLION
November 30, 1974

One afternoon in 1968, Marva Drew's son came home from school sniveling: a heartless teacher had told him that it was impossible to count to a million.

Marva decided to show her son that nothing was impossible. The 51-year-old Iowa housewife fed a sheet of paper into a Royal upright and began to type: 1 . . . 2 . . . 3 . . .

For the next six years, Marva devoted 8 tedious hours a day to her project, clacking away early in the morning before work, and late into the night before bed. She burned through 12 typewriter ribbons, five reams of paper, and her own physical health. It was not the key tapping so much as the carriage returns—hundreds of thousands of them—that caused the most pain. Besides that, there were the bouts of insomnia in which monospaced serif integers crawled across the page of her eyelids whenever she lay down to sleep. "That last 100,000 I was ready to throw in the towel," she said.

On November 30, 1974, after thousands of hours of patient work, Marva typed out her final entry: 1,000,000. "You just don't realize what a million really is," she said, tapping the 10-inch stack on her desk.

In 1993, an unemployed Maryland man surpassed Marva's feat of endurance: He typewrote all the numerals to 1,000,001.

BREATHLESS
December 1, 1997

On this day, legendary saxophonist Kenny G set a record for the longest note ever held on a sax when he sustained an E-flat for 45 minutes and 47 seconds using a technique called circular breathing (made famous by jazz reedman Rahsaan Roland Kirk). Incidentally, Kenny's other world record, for bestselling instrumental album of all time, is for 1992's *Breathless*.

AGAINST THE WIND
December 2, 1979

A century after a rogue breeze spoiled Sarah Ann Henley's suicidal leap (*see May 8*), another timely gust thwarted the suicide of Elvita Adams from New York's Empire State Building. On December 2, 1979, Adams, a 29-year-old Bronx woman, entered the skyscraper's 86th-floor observatory, scaled a seven-foot spiked fence, and jumped. She fell about 20 feet before a strong gale blew her back onto a concrete ledge on the 85th floor, where she landed with a broken pelvis. A security guard pulled her in through a window before she could try again.

I DON'T KNOW MUCH ABOUT ART, BUT I KNOW WHEN IT'S UPSIDE-DOWN
December 3, 1961

When it comes to abstract art, even the experts sometimes can't tell up from down. In October 1961, New York's Museum of Modern Art opened an exhibit on the French abstract artist Henri Matisse, unaware that one of the compositions on display—a paper-cut collage of a sailboat and its reflection—had been hung upside down.

For 47 days, visitors walked past *Le Bateau* (1953), oblivious to the blunder. (Even Matisse's own son, Pierre, missed it.) Of all people, it was a Wall Street stockbroker who came to the boat's rescue. Studying the work, Genevieve Habert reasoned that the crisper, sharper image of the sailboat should logically be on top, while the softer, blurred image would be its watery reflection below. On December 3, 1961, Habert alerted museum authorities. After one glance, the director of exhibitions cried, "Oh no! It shouldn't be hung this way." He promptly flipped the painting 180 degrees.

An assistant curator accepted blame for the error but claimed she'd been misled by screw holes on the back of the frame, which were positioned at the wrong end. Clearly, the boat had been capsized before.

A WILDE DESIRE
December 4, 1878

A literary love rivalry came to an end on this day when Bram Stoker, author of *Dracula,* married Florence Balcombe, an Irish beauty he'd stolen away from Oscar Wilde earlier that year.

Stoker and Wilde both met Balcombe around the same time in 1875 and fell instantly and madly in love with her. "[She is] exquisitely pretty," Wilde wrote in a letter to a friend, ". . . just seventeen with the most perfectly beautiful face I ever saw and not a sixpence of money." Balcombe began dating Wilde, but soon grew uninterested in the impoverished dandy and dumped him. Months later, she was engaged to Stoker.

When Wilde heard the news of her betrothal, he was devastated. He mailed back all the letters Balcombe had written him ("how strange and out of tune it all reads now"), and requested that she return a gold cross he'd given her "one Christmas morning long ago." In part to avoid reminders of his heartbreak, he left the lovebirds in Ireland and moved away to England, where he lived and wrote principally for the rest of his life.

LITTLE PRINTS
December 5, 1996

Despite being separated by 70 million years of evolution, koalas and humans have nearly identical fingerprints. Maciej Henneberg, a forensic scientist and University of Adelaide professor, noticed the likeness while handling koalas in Urimbirra Wildlife Park, in Australia. He announced his findings on December 5, 1996, along with a warning to criminal investigators to begin expanding their suspect pools: "Although it is extremely unlikely that koala prints would be found at the scene of a crime," Henneberg said, "police should at least be aware of the possibility."

MODERN FAMILY COURT
December 6, 2016

In a lawsuit filed in Louisiana on this day, Colombian American actress Sofía Vergara became the first person to be sued by her own embryos.

The suit, brought by Vergara's ex-fiancé Nick Loeb in an effort to gain custody of their frozen embryos, contended that "Emma" and "Isabella" (the "plaintiffs") have the right to be born and claim an inheritance. Loeb cleverly filed the suit in Louisiana, a state where fertilized eggs are considered juridical persons, even though the plaintiffs resided in a fertility clinic in Beverly Hills, California.

Loeb's claim to Louisiana jurisdiction was a stretch: according to the suit, it was the last state where the embryos' life was secure and viable, since Vergara broke up with Loeb at Louis Armstrong New Orleans International Airport.

NO HE DOESN'T
December 7, 1975

On this day, Barry Manilow reached #1 on the Billboard adult contemporary charts with his hit "I Write the Songs," a song he didn't write.

When producer Clive Davis first brought the tune to Manilow, the pop star worried he would seem insincere or narcissistic. "Here's a song that I didn't even write, and yet I'm declaring that I write the songs that make the whole world sing?" At the time, the 32-year-old artist fancied himself a singer-songwriter in the vein of a Billy Joel or Elton John, not a cover crooner in the tradition of Sinatra, but Davis had time and again suppressed Manilow's songwriting ambition; for him to then bring Manilow a tune called "I Write the Songs" was the ultimate insult.

In the end, "I Write the Songs" became Manilow's signature number. It won a Grammy for Song of the Year in 1977, and *Billboard* ranked it the thirteenth best song of 1976. Nobody cared that the man who "wrote it" didn't write it.

MOTHER MARY
December 8, 1726

For three wild months in 1726, England was gripped by the case of Mary Toft, a twenty-five-year-old peasant from Surrey who gave birth to rabbits.

The strange saga began in September when Mary, alone in her house, cried out suddenly in labor pain. A neighbor rushed over in time to see Mary push out a formless slop of animal parts, among which was a pig's bladder, a cat's paw, and a half-grown, stillborn rabbit. The neighbor sent for John Howard, a local obstetrician, who tended to Mary while the animal births continued into the night.

Over the next month, Howard delivered Mary of a dozen more rabbits. He pickled them in jars of alcohol and invited doctors from all around Europe to study them. In a letter to a prominent English physician, Howard describes the hectic scene:

> I have taken or deliver'd the poor Woman of three more
> Rabbets, all three half grown, one of them a dunn Rabbet;
> the last leap'd twenty three Hours in the Uterus before it dy'd.
> As soon as the eleventh Rabbet was taken away, up leap'd
> the twelfth Rabbet, which is now leaping. If you have any
> curious Person that is pleased to come Post, may see another
> leap in her Uterus, and shall take it from her if he pleases . . .
> I do not know how many Rabbets may be behind.

News spread fast and Mary became a local celebrity. That her name was Mary, and that she conceived immaculately, lent the story an air of biblical truth that attracted many faithful believers. But Mary had her skeptics, too. That December, a group of scientists put Mary under round-the-clock observation. The rabbit births suddenly ceased. A few days later, a porter was caught trying to sneak a rabbit into Mary's room.

Mary was taken into custody, and she held out through two days of interrogation. Finally, on December 8, 1726, after a surgeon threatened to perform a painful surgery, she formally confessed: she had been sticking rabbits up there for months.

Mary was charged with being a "Notorious and Vile Cheat" and sent to Bridewell Prison, where her warders exhibited her to fervid crowds eager to see the woman who had deceived England for months.

AHEAD OF ITS TIME
December 9, 1868

The world's first traffic light was installed in London on December 9, 1868—18 years before the automobile was invented.

The gas-lit lamp controlled horse-drawn traffic at the busy junction of Bridge Street, Parliament Street, and Great George Street, outside the Houses of Parliament. It was operated by a police constable, who manually alternated colored lenses on a Victorian lantern to moderate traffic flow—green for go, red for stop.

The light exploded three weeks later when its gas line sprung a leak. The cop at post was badly burned and the new traffic management system was abandoned. It would be 60 years before traffic lights returned to London.

THE FIRST FEMALE PALEONTOLOGIST
December 10, 1823

Mary Anning grew up in Lyme Regis, on England's rocky southern coast, and spent most of her childhood combing the beach for shells and pebbles. Her father was a commercial "curios" salesman; he ran a seaside stand selling geological souvenirs found in the sand or in the nearby limestone cliffs. He died when Mary was eleven, leaving her and her mother to run the business.

On December 10, 1823, while out searching for specimens in the stratified bluffs, Anning spotted something no human had ever seen before. It was the skeleton of a monster nine feet long, a perplexing hybridized beast composed of—in the words of the French naturalist Georges Cuvier—"a lizard's head, a crocodile's teeth, a trunk and tail like an ordinary quadruped, a chameleon's ribs, a whale's paddles" and an enormous neck that looked "like a serpent tacked on to the body."

It was a Plesiosaurs, an aquatic dinosaur of the early Jurassic, and the first complete specimen of its kind ever found. At a time when the word "dinosaur" didn't yet exist, Anning's discovery baffled the scientific community and ignited in her a passion for ancient life. She taught herself all the sciences—geology, biology, archaeology—and went on to become one of the most prolific paleontologists of her day.

It was only after her death, in 1847, that she received her due credit, helped along by Charles Dickens (one of her biggest advocates), as well as by a popular nursery rhyme—"She sells seashells by the seashore"—a tongue twister based on the life and work of the world's first female paleontologist.

HOUSTON, WE HAVE A PROBLEM . . .
December 11, 1998

On this day, NASA scientists launched the Mars Climate Orbiter on a nine-month journey to study the Martian climate. It was doomed before it even left the ground.

Unknown to NASA at the time, one of the engineering teams working on the project had performed its trajectory calculations using English units (pound-seconds) while another team had used metric units (newton-seconds). When the Orbiter reached the Red Planet a year later, it skimmed too close to the atmosphere and disintegrated.

Cost of the botched mission: $327.6 million.

GRANDFATHERED IN
December 12, 1866

On this day, the *Wilmington Daily Dispatch* reported on the bizarre case of William Harmon, a Pennsylvania man who through a series of marital entanglements had become his own grandfather. Harmon explained the circumstances in a letter:

> *I married a widow who had a grown-up daughter. My father visited our house very often, fell in love with my step-daughter and married her. So my father became my son-in-law, and my step-daughter my mother, because she was my father's wife. Sometime afterward my wife had a son; he was my father's brother-in-law, and my uncle for he was the brother of my stepmother. My father's wife—i.e., my stepmother—had also a son; he was, of course, my brother, and in the meantime my grandchild, for he was the son of my daughter. My wife was my grandmother, because she was my mother's mother. I was my wife's husband and grandchild at the same time. And as the husband of a person's grandmother is his grandfather, I am my own grandfather.*

HIS (NOT SO) FINEST HOUR
December 13, 1931

Mario Contasino, an unemployed mechanic from Yonkers, accidentally struck and nearly killed Winston Churchill while driving down New York's Fifth Avenue at 10:30 p.m. on this night.

As he exited his taxi, Churchill looked left for oncoming traffic. Seeing no southbound headlights, the British statesman forged ahead, forgetting that traffic in America moves on the right. He was hit by Contasino's car and dragged several yards. "I do not understand why I was not broken like an eggshell or squashed like a gooseberry," Churchill later wrote. The mechanic put Churchill's bloodied body into his backseat and drove him to Lenox Hill Hospital three blocks away, where he was treated for cuts, bruises, and a shoulder sprain.

There *was* one upside to it all. Churchill's physician, Otto C. Pickhardt, wrote him a note certifying "that the post-accident convalescence of Hon. Winston S. Churchill necessitates the use of alcoholic spirits especially at meal times. The quantity is naturally indefinite." A doctor's note was one of the few legal exceptions to America's ban on alcohol during Prohibition.

ROYAL STALKER
December 14, 1838

On this day, 14-year-old Edward Jones snuck into Buckingham Palace disguised as a chimney sweep. He entered the queen's empty bedroom, poked around her personal effects, pocketed some letters and coins, and was finally seen peeking into the chamber of a night porter. Jones led an impressive chase through the palace and might have escaped but for a trail of soot he left behind from his disguise. The prints led the porter to the Marble Hall, where he caught the intruder hiding behind a pillar with Queen Victoria's underwear stuffed down his pants.

PATENT IRONY
December 15, 1836

The first fire hydrant is credited to Frederick Graff Sr., a 26-year-old hydraulic engineer with the Philadelphia Water Works, but his claim will never be verified: his patent for the fire hydrant was lost in a patent office fire.

On December 15, 1836, a blaze tore through the U.S. Patent Office, wiping out some 10,000 records. Though some American cities had already adopted Graff's hydrant design—a two-foot standpipe with pressurized water, in a state of permanent readiness—Washington was behind the times. The U.S. capital still relied on fireplugs, direct taps into underground water mains that first had to be dug into, then drilled, then siphoned, before water could be conveyed toward a fire. By the time the firefighters began their assembly line of sloshing buckets, the patent office was already engulfed in flames.

AND THE $64,000 QUESTION IS . . .
December 16, 1955

On this day, American talk show psychologist Dr. Joyce Brothers became the only woman ever to win the top prize on the game show *The $64,000 Question*.

The producers deliberately tried to stump Brothers by asking about the manliest subject they could fathom. For her $64,000 question, Brothers was asked to name the year, city, winner, manner of winning, and number of rounds of each of three obscure boxing matches from the previous three decades. She aced it.

A BRIDGE TO SELL
December 17, 1928

George C. Parker was the most successful con man ever to walk the earth and try to sell you a piece of it. During his thirty years plying his trade in New York, Parker "sold" unwary immigrants the Statue of Liberty, the Metropolitan Museum of Art, Grant's Tomb, the Brooklyn Bridge, and other city landmarks he never actually owned. (The Brooklyn Bridge was his favorite product to hawk: he sold it nearly 60 times.) His exploits gave rise to the expression "And if you believe that, I have a bridge to sell you," a popular way to tease someone for their gullibility. He was finally put away in Sing Sing prison (that's one landmark he never sold) for life on December 17, 1928, where his tales of con-artistry made him a legend among his fellow inmates.

SPEED WARS
December 18, 1898

On a deserted stretch of road near Paris, Count Gaston de Chasseloup-Laubat, a French aristocrat, set the world's first land speed record in a battery-powered Jeantaud Duc car. His time: 39.24 mph.

The record didn't last a month. In January 1899, his rival, the Belgian racecar driver Camille Jenatzy, pushed the mark to 41.42 mph. Two hours after that, Chasseloup-Laubat upped it to 43.69 mph. Ten days later, Jenatzy threw down a 49.93 mph run. Back and forth it went for the next three months, in a highly publicized speed war that captivated all of France. The Belgian, at last, emerged the victor: in April, Jenatzy blazed down the racecourse at 65.79 mph inside a souped-up, sanded down speed mobile that looked as lean and mean as a torpedo.

The real winner of the French-Belgian speed war of 1899 was the electric car. The battery-powered, emission-free vehicles used by Jenatzy and Chasseloup-Laubat proved both faster and cleaner than the noisy gas-powered alternative. That summer, Paris adopted a fleet of electric taxis, and half a world away, New York did the same.

Then in August 1902, an internal combustion automobile driven by William Vanderbilt II, of the prominent American Vanderbilt family, clocked a time of 76.08 mph. Unable to meet the world's need for speed, the electric car soon died out.

THE TOILET PAPER PANIC OF '73
December 19, 1973

1973 was a year of shortages in the United States. Oil, electricity, and even onions suffered periods of limited supply, and by year's end American consumers had developed a "shortage psychology"—a trigger response to buy and hoard supplies at the slightest scare.

Then along came *Tonight Show* host Johnny Carson and an ill-timed joke:

> *"You know, we've got all sorts of shortages these days. But have you heard the latest? I'm not kidding. I saw it in the papers. There's a shortage of toilet paper."*

Carson was referring to a report that pulp production had decreased at a few Wisconsin paper mills—hardly cause for national concern. He thought it would get a few laughs. Instead it caused a national panic.

The next day, Americans went on an apocalyptic toilet paper shopping spree. They stripped markets to the shelf, and storeowners shrewdly hiked up prices to capitalize on the sudden demand. "I heard it on the news, so I bought 15 extra rolls," one Texas woman told *The New York Times*. When asked what guests should bring to her baby shower, a panicked Pennsylvanian replied, "Toilet paper."

Carson went on the air later that week to assure Americans that TP was in full stock. The only problem was—now it wasn't. The week's buying binge had run supermarkets dry. Carson's joke had caused an actual toilet paper shortage.

The toilet paper economy struggled for the next month, before finally righting itself in early 1974. It would be another few weeks before toilet paper consumption returned to pre-Carson levels.

WELL DAMN
December 20

The first casualty of the Hoover Dam project—one of the largest public works projects ever undertaken on American soil—was J. G. Tierney, a surveyor with the Bureau of Reclamation, sent to conduct a preliminary assessment of the dam site. On December 20, 1922, while balancing on a barge in the Colorado River, Tierney fell into the water and drowned. The last to die on the project, coincidentally, was Tierney's son, Patrick Tierney. He fell from one of the dam's 338-foot-tall intake towers on December 20, 1935—exactly thirteen years after his father's death.

TOSSING AND TURNING
December 21, 1889

On this day, a fidgety burglar was sentenced to San Quentin prison for ten years after he was caught hiding under his former employer's bed armed with a pistol and a bottle of chloroform.

Having grown uncomfortable in his position in the middle of the night, Joseph Blackman—who had been fired from his dishwashing job the previous week for flirting with his employer's wife—attempted to turn over and struck the bed with his shoulder.

His squirming awoke the man above him, who, according to a report, "gave his former dishwasher a good drubbing" until police arrived. When asked, Blackman could give no reasonable explanation for why he went under the bed, or what he planned to do when he came out.

A GIFT TO TREASURE
December 22, 1937

Hitler might have paid lip service to the annihilation of American culture, but in private he was actually a big fan of Walt Disney—particularly that little mascot mouse. For Christmas 1937, Nazi propaganda minister Joseph Goebbels gave Adolf Hitler a gift of 18 Mickey Mouse films, imported direct from America. The *Führer* "is very excited," Goebbels wrote in his December 22 diary entry. "He is completely happy about this treasure."

HIDE NOR HAIR
December 23, 1975

So popular was the "comb-over" hairstyle in the 1970s that two men tried to copyright it. In a patent application filed on December 23, 1975, Donald J. Smith and his partly balding father, Frank, describe the classic method for concealing male pattern baldness:

> *[The process requires] separating the hair on the head into several substantially equal sections, taking the hair on one section and placing it over the bald area, then taking the hair on another section and placing it over the first section, and finally taking the hair on the remaining sections and placing it over the other sections whereby the bald area will be completely covered.*

Two years later, the Smiths received U.S. Patent 4,022,227 for the comb-over.

O CHRISTMAS TREE
December 24, 1832

Christmas trees were introduced to the English-speaking world when the Duchess of Kent had one placed in the room of her 13-year-old daughter, Victoria, the future Queen of England. Victoria wrote about it in her journal entry of December 24, 1832:

> *After Mamma had rung a bell 3 times we went in. There were two large round tables on which were placed two trees hung with lights and sugar ornaments. All the presents being placed round the tree. I had one table for myself and the Conroy family had the other together.*

The tradition of decorating Christmas trees came from Germany, as did Victoria's mother, grandmother, and future husband. When Victoria married Prince Albert, he ordered evergreens from his homeland and decorated them as he had done as a child. He wrote in 1847 that he hoped his children's enjoyment of "Christmas-trees is not less than ours used to be."

O CHRISTMAS TRUCE
December 25, 1914

For one day, World War I hostilities ceased in the spirit of Christmas. At dawn on this day, soldiers emerged from their trenches and crossed "no man's land" to exchange gifts and goodwill with their enemies. German and British joined together to sing carols, break bread, and pose for photos. Several soldiers struck up an impromptu game of soccer, and one German barber gave his prewar British patron a complimentary haircut.

GUARDIAN OF THE LANGUAGE
December 26, 1777

Dolly Pentreath, assumed to be the last fluent speaker of ancient Cornish, died in her home in Mousehole, England, on December 26, 1777, taking the language with her into extinction. Her defiant last words were, "Me ne vidn cewsel Sawznek!"—"I don't want to speak English!"

The 85-year-old fishmonger had a reputation for cursing people out in long streams of incomprehensible profanity during moments of anger. When Daines Barrington, an English linguist, came to Mousehole looking for the legendary guardian of Cornish, Pentreath unleashed upon him, "in an angry tone of voice of two or three minutes," a torrent of linguistic abuse in her expiring tongue. When one day a man knocked over her fish basket in the marketplace, she pronounced him "Kronek hager du!"—"An ugly black toad!"

THE OLD PHILADELPHIA LADY
December 27, 1899

The most prolific contributor to the Paris *Herald* was an anonymous woman known as the "Old Philadelphia Lady." She published her first Letter to the Editor on December 27, 1899:

To the Editor of the Herald:

I am anxious to find out the way to figure the temperature from centigrade to Fahrenheit and vice versa. In other words, I want to know, whenever I see the temperature designated on the centigrade thermometer, how to find out what it would be on Fahrenheit's thermometer.

Old Philadelphia Lady

James Gordon Bennett Jr., the *Herald*'s eccentric publisher, ran the letter again in the paper the next day—and the day after that—and every day afterward for 18 years. So long as readers continued to respond to the letter, Bennett continued to publish it. All told, the Fahrenheit-confounded Philadelphian appeared in the newspaper 6,718 times. Bennett defended her to the last: "Whoever interferes with or suppresses the Old Philadelphia Lady," he told his staff, "ceases automatically all connection with the *Herald*."

JUST SHOOT ME
December 28, 1918

As a member of the Irish Citizen Army, Constance Markievicz participated in the 1916 Easter Rising, an armed insurrection by Irish republicans to cast off British rule. She was caught and condemned to death by firing squad, but the Court reduced her sentence to life imprisonment, a mercy she did not want. When informed of her commutation, she told the officer, "I do wish your lot had the decency to shoot me."

Markievicz ran for the House of Commons from her prison cell in 1918 as a candidate for the Sinn Féin Party and, on December 28, she won, becoming the first woman ever elected to Parliament. She, of course, never took her seat: while her colleagues convened at Westminster Palace, Markievicz was behind bars four miles away, a political prisoner of the government she tried to overthrow—and had just been elected to.

THE BRAHE WAY
December 29, 1566

Danish astronomer Tycho Brahe came from a family of hard-drinking, quick-tempered duelists. He lost four cousins to impetuous dueling (two of them killed by other family members), and Tycho seemed destined to lose at least a part of himself the same way.

During a holiday party on December 29, 1566, the twenty-year-old astronomy student fell into an argument with a classmate—who also, not surprisingly, was his third cousin—and they decided to settle it the ol' Brahe way. The cousins took up broadswords, and Brahe lost half his nose. For the rest of his life, he would wear a gold prosthetic to cover up his deformity.

TIME TRAVEL
December 30, 2011

This date never occurred in Samoa. At the stroke of midnight on December 29, the island nation skipped forward in time to December 31, bypassing December 30 entirely.

The move was designed to improve Samoa's trade relations by aligning its time zone with that of its western neighbors, Australia and New Zealand. Incidentally, it also shook up Samoa's relationship with its eastern neighbor, *American* Samoa, a U.S. territory that chose to remain in Samoa Standard Time rather than cross over to the new West Samoa Time. The two Samoas—visible to each other on a clear day—are now a full day apart. In an afternoon's boat ride, a Samoan can move one day forward or backward in time.

PLAN BIG
December 31, 1759

Arthur Guinness was one optimistic businessman. On New Year's Eve 1759, the future beer baron signed a lease on a defunct brewery in Dublin for the term length of 9,000 years and started brewing his famous dark stout. It remains the longest land lease ever recorded.

The agreement—a four-page run-on sentence of the obscurest legalese—also guaranteed Guinness free use of the city's water supply. When Dublin officials, in 1775, demanded Guinness begin paying a levy for access to clean water, the brewer struck a deal for water rights at an annual sum of £10—for a lease term of 8,795 years. The man sure liked to plan for the future.

ACKNOWLEDGMENTS

Many wonderful, patient people served to help this book along. For their personal and professional support, I owe particular thanks to Andrea Morris, Maureen Maryanski, Benjamin Levinsohn, Elizabeth Ziman, Flavia Salama, Martha Mihalick, Camille Cauti, Jason Baker, Scott Messina, Lizz Brady, Jo Fagan, Kaethe Fine, Anna Ziering, Denise Oswald, Daniel Rosenberg, Steve Mockus, and Amanda Simpson Neill, all of whom contributed generously to this project in ways big and small.

I'm also indebted to my fellow collectors of historical miscellany, whose exhaustive (and exhausting, certainly) research helped pave the way for this book, and whose works served as a constant reminder that such a thing was possible: Greg Ross, William Hartston, Elizabeth and Gerald Donaldson, Charles Panati, and Ken Jennings.

A special note of thanks also to Sharon Lustbader, who first sparked my interest in writing, and to Michael J. Fine, who first gave that spark its kindling. If this book should become a hot seller, they are the arsonists responsible.

And, lastly, a sincere apology to all my softball teammates whom I neglected in the championship season to finish up work on this book. Sorry, guys.

ABOUT THE AUTHOR

Gabe Henry is a New York-based writer and former staff member of the New-York Historical Society who has written on subjects ranging from history and science to art, sports, music, and popular culture. He lives in Brooklyn.

ABOUT THE ILLUSTRATOR

Dave Hopkins is an artist whose work has appeared in magazines from the *Economist* to *MOJO*, as well as product packaging, advertising, and numerous books. He lives in the UK.

INDEX